Inspirational – and Cautionary – Tales for Would-be School Leaders

Based upon Gerald Haigh's acclaimed weekly column in *The Times Educational Supplement*, this book is a lively and refreshing look at what it takes to get on in teaching. Over recent years Haigh's columns – 'Second Half', for experienced teachers, and 'Leading Questions', specifically for teachers in leadership positions – have developed a loyal following from readers. This reworked and carefully selected collection will give leaders and aspiring leaders in education vital insights and observations into a wide range of topics including:

- the recruitment game
- building your career
- dealing with people, making mistakes and learning
- lessons from heroes and gurus – from Tom Peters and Peter Drucker to Lawrence of Arabia
- supporting colleagues
- getting a life beyond school.

Touching on everything from the experiences of acclaimed head teachers such as Sir Robert Salisbury, to the film *The Caine Mutiny*, the author's incisive eye will give teachers wanting to get on in their careers both inspiration and much to ponder upon.

Gerald Haigh is an educational writer and consultant specialising in school management matters. He has a background of teaching and leadership in a wide range of schools.

Inspirational – and Cautionary – Tales for Would-be School Leaders

Gerald Haigh

LONDON AND NEW YORK

First published 2008 by Routledge

2 Park Square, Milton Park, Abingdon, Oxfordshire OX14 4RN
605 Third Avenue, New York, NY 10017

Routledge is an imprint of the Taylor & Francis Group, an informa business

First issued in hardback 2020

Copyright © 2008 Gerald Haigh

All rights reserved. No part of this book may be reprinted or reproduced or utilised in any form or by any electronic, mechanical, or other means, now known or hereafter invented, including photocopying and recording, or in any information storage or retrieval system, without permission in writing from the publishers.

Notice:
Product or corporate names may be trademarks or registered trademarks, and are used only for identification and explanation without intent to infringe.

Typeset in Times by
GreenGate Publishing Services, Tonbridge, Kent

British Library Cataloguing in Publication Data
A catalogue record for this book is available from the British Library

Library of Congress Cataloging-in-Publication Data
Haigh, Gerald.
Inspirational – and cautionary – tales for would-be school leaders / Gerald Haigh.
p. cm.
ISBN 978-0-415-43790-5 (hardback) -- ISBN 978-0-415-43792-9 (pbk.) -- ISBN 978-0-203-93306-0 (e-book) 1. Educational leadership. 2. School management and organization. 3. Teaching--Vocational guidance. I. Title.
LB2806.4.H35 2008
371.2--dc22
2007027628

ISBN 13: 978–0–415–43790–5 (hbk)
ISBN 13: 978–0–415–43792–9 (pbk)
ISBN 13: 978–0–203–93306–0 (ebk)

Contents

Introduction	1
Improvement might come at a price	4
Finding the oil on the track	6
Delegation's not just letting go	9
Slow but sure	12
Just tell them what to do	15
Dealing with the maverick team member	18
Epiphany moments	21
Think about the impression you're making	24
Things to do	26
Small beginnings	28
Don't interfere when they know what they're doing	31
Be open to bad news	33
Don't assume the other person's job is better	36
If they don't get it, just tell them	39
Leadership role models	41
Leave room for the oddball	43
Don't say 'tell me' unless you mean it	45
Sense and nonsense in time management	47
Status doesn't always come with competence	49
Leaders under pressure may be signalling for help	51
Listen impartially	54
Make sure the message is clear	57
Calling it a team doesn't make it one	60
Hierarchy shouldn't breed distance	63

Job satisfaction really does count	65
Let people out of their ruts occasionally	68
Every member of staff matters equally	70
Build on strengths	72
Focus on the key skills when you build your team	75
Listening and really listening	77
Valuing your people	80
Good teachers have lives beyond the job	82
Making best use of people	84
Handling a star in the team	86
The new broom might not be the right tool	89
Make sure your people have home lives	91
Do senior leadership figures need to teach in class?	94
You can't always achieve perfection	96
You learn some things very quickly	98
Don't assume everyone thinks like you	101
Offering more work, but no more money	104
Moving on from headship	106
Managing an impossible staff member	109
Don't use the school to indulge your personal skills	111
Spreading the concept of leadership	114
Leadership in the classroom	116
The staffroom tells a story about the school	119
Are you a different person at home?	121
Keeping ahead of the job	124
Maybe it's the system that's wrong	126
What sort of manager are you?	129
Get the details right	132
The man who invented management	135
Performance-related pay might not work	138
It's easy to be distracted from the core activity	141
Put your effort in the right place	143
Settle down for the long haul	145
Slow down and be aware of your good fortune	148
Help your leaders to lead	151

Introduction

When I embarked on my leadership column in *The Times Educational Supplement* I wondered long and hard how to approach it. I knew I had useful things to say to people currently working in schools. Quite aside from my own long experience of teaching and headship, my many assignments for the *TES* and other journals and organisations have for years put me in continuous contact with education at every level, from the classroom and the head's study to the government offices where policies were formed.

How, though, to say something helpful without seeming to preach or state the obvious?

The answer, I realised, was simply to tell some stories. I like stories, I enjoy telling them, and I believe that religious leaders haven't been story-tellers by accident. They've always known that the way to reach a person's soul, as it were, is through a good story.

Stories would also enable me to concentrate on people rather than systems or policies. We're always interested in people. We want to hear about the ones who are brave, successful, resourceful, imaginative, creative. But we also, because we're human, want to hear about those who are over-ambitious, greedy, arrogant and inept. There's something to learn from all of them, including some who exist only in the pages of fiction or on the screen.

Perhaps most importantly of all, I wanted to entertain and amuse. So much of what's written about education is worthy and serious. I was keen to do something different. Yes, I wanted to make points, but I thought that in the end if someone read one of my columns and took away from it nothing more than a chuckle and a nod of recognition – a bit of relief from a pressured life – then I'd settle for that.

So, in my columns, I began to tell stories. Some of them I knew already – I was sure, too, that my readers would be familiar with at least some of them. Many others were new to me, culled from every conceivable published and unpublished resource as well as from my own experience. In every case, though, I tried to make a connection that would light up something in that bit of the reader's mind where he or she was thinking about the job of running a school. Maybe it would give pause for thought, or cause somebody to revise an approach. Perhaps it would just provide a moment's entertainment, or even a spark of anger. I didn't pretend that I'd bring about fundamental change. Just so long as a bit of a connection was made, I'd be content.

So, here are my stories – and as it happens, most of them do turn out to be about people. Sometimes they're real people in the literal sense; sometimes though real to me, they're actually fictional, if you see what I mean. I've grown to be very familiar with them as I've planned this book, and I know you'll be intrigued by them: you'll meet Bud Holland playing fast and loose with his giant bomber, 'Chainsaw' Al Dunlap cutting a swathe through the workforce in pursuit of excellence, Ernest Shackleton leading his men to safety and A.J. Wentworth struggling to control his boys at Burgrove Prep School.

Only now, incidentally, with the articles lined up before me as it were, do I realise how my choice of characters betrays my areas of interest. You will find here, for example, two admirals – one who swears and one who sinks – several sea captains, an air force pilot. There are very few sports persons on the other hand – though the great Puskas puts in a cameo appearance, as does Sir Stirling Moss.

There are some management gurus in these pages, too. There's a school of thought that the average guru is someone who builds a reputation by stating the obvious in portentous language. To some extent that's true. It's also true, though, that the obvious sometimes needs stating, with clarity and emphasis. Someone once said, of rocket science, something like this – 'Safety in the space programme is a matter of identifying the basics and getting them right. It isn't rocket science.'

You'll also detect where my professional and leadership sympathies lie. I'm for collaboration, humane values, seeking the best in people and building on their strengths. Good school leaders are always aware of the need to match their actions and intentions to the values they're trying to nurture in children and young people.

Almost every one of the pieces has appeared in some form on the leadership pages of the *TES*. A few were used elsewhere in the same journal, and just one or two have been specially written, although to the same brief. In a number of cases, freed from the space restrictions of a weekly newspaper, I've taken the opportunity to develop an argument a little more, or add some details. I've also done some tweaking in places where a reference or an anecdote seems too dependent on the reader knowing what was in the news at the time the piece was written. Mostly though, apart from a few lines of introduction, the columns are as they were in the paper – they seem to sit quite comfortably at their original length.

Improvement might come at a price

School improvement is very high on everyone's agenda.
What used to be the 'school development plan' has metamorphosed into the 'school improvement plan'.
That's fine, but doubts arise when the definition of 'improvement' becomes a narrow one, based exclusively on measured performance results – exam and test scores, attendance figures and the like. It's just possible that too narrow a focus leads to problems in other areas. That's certainly the case in the example I use here, taken from the harsh world of American business.

A few months after I became a head, I asked the local authority advisory team to inspect our school. In the days before regular and frequent inspections, it was a good pre-emptive ploy, because it was then very possible to go for a very long time without ever being scrutinised from outside. Which was fine, except that when the inspectors did finally arrive, everyone may well have been in for a shock.

So asking for an inspection, quite early on my headship, was a precautionary move. It would also, I believe, add weight to the changes I was proposing to make, because the authority would presumably agree with them – they had interviewed me after all.

So the team arrived and wandered around for a day. Then the chief primary adviser came to see me.

'You've turned it around', he said.

I have to say I was quite taken aback by that. 'Improved things a bit'? Maybe. 'Made a decent start'? Perhaps. But 'turned it around'? I'm not sure about that even now. It sounded considerably more radical than anything I would myself have concluded.

That notion of 'turning round' is heard even more in these days of our preoccupation with measurable school improvement. There are heads who are reputedly good at it, moving from school to school, shoving them one by one up the league tables.

Let's hope, though, that they do not cleave too assiduously to the methods of 'Chainsaw' Al Dunlap, the self-styled 'turnaround king.'

Dunlap, a renowned chief executive officer (CEO) in the States, went into companies with one aim in mind – to improve what for him was the single key measure of performance, namely shareholder value. If the share price went up significantly he was succeeding. If it went down, or stayed the same, or even if it only went up a bit, he was failing. And failing was not something he was in the habit of doing. In a typical example, the share price of a business he ran rose from $1.77 to $18.55 in the two-and-a-half years he was there.

How did he do it? There's no mystery. In fact it wasn't even very difficult. All Chainsaw Al did was focus single-mindedly on that one important target. Anything else was fair game for being cut, sidelined, and covered up. So, in one case he stopped the company's charitable donations, closed two factories and, crucially, slashed the research and development budget. One senior manager recalls being told by the jolly Al:

'We don't want any bullshit. Your life depends on hitting that number.'

The shareholders, and Wall Street, loved it. The feelings of the sacked workers (11,000 in one company alone) can only be guessed at.

Of course, in the end, it all fell apart, and it was Al's turn to be fired. There was no real long-term thinking, you see. It was all about chasing a target and not worrying about real, deep-seated and sustained development.

Heads, of course, even turnaround kings, don't work like that. If they were entirely focused on improving their GCSE As to Cs for example, then they might, for example, identify those children whose results could conceivably be lifted from C to B, and give them special intensive work, spending less time on the ones who were either safely in the B zone, or irrevocably among the Cs. But that would be entirely wrong, wouldn't it, and no self-respecting school leadership would do that. Would they?

I suppose, in fact, that a few schools have done that – or something mildly of that nature anyway. It's not common though. The fact that school leaders do generally behave honourably around narrow targets owes everything to their integrity and values and not much to the system within which they're expected to work.

Finding the oil on the track

Great sportsmen and women know when to take risks and when not, when to push and when to let someone else take the strain for a bit. Sir Stirling Moss, widely acknowledged as Britain's greatest racing driver, had that mix of caution and courage, which is why he's still with us of course.

That same understanding of when to be at the cutting edge and when to be a bit more circumspect is one of the keys to success in leadership, which is why I use here a story about Sir Stirling to make the point.

After you, Masten

Sir Stirling Moss, born in 1929, is, at the time of writing, still hale and hearty and driving quickly at exhibition events. He survived an era when too many of his contemporaries were being killed. Part of the explanation is that he knew when to take risks and when not. For example, after one race, people wondered why Moss had spent a lot of time behind Masten Gregory, an able and occasionally over-eager driver, but not in Stirling's class. Moss smiled.

'It was slippery,' he said. 'So I thought, "Let old Masten find the oil".' (Masten did have more accidents than Stirling, and had a peculiar habit of jumping out of the car just before it crashed, twice being seriously injured doing it. He eventually retired, became a diamond merchant and died peacefully in his bed.)

It can be a bit like that in school. It's good to be on the cutting edge of innovation, but it is possible to reach a little too far and start hitting the oil patches. Nothing, in my opinion, better demonstrates this than the difficulty schools can encounter when they move too quickly in installing computer software. I visited a school once in which one of the coffee mugs in the staffroom belonged to a technician from the firm supplying the computerised registration system.

'He's here so often he's included in the coffee club', commented the deputy head.

The school, I discovered, had decided to move from traditional paper attendance registers to a system using small portable computers in the classroom. It was a seemingly simple idea. A teacher called up the register on the screen – it arrived by wireless connection from the central computer in the office. She then called the register, marking off absentees on the screen with the keyboard, then pressed a key to send the completed register, again by wireless link, down to the school office.

Now, with more and more schools fully networked, and teachers equipped with laptops or handheld computers, systems like this are much more common. This school, though, was something of a pioneer, and as such, unsurprisingly, it was finding the snags, the oil on the track.

It wasn't so much that there were problems with the software, but that the management team had made a calculated decision to make the change quickly across the whole school. The system was installed during July, and on the first day of term in September every single form tutor was faced with the electronic gadget, having had a brief introduction before the holiday.

Well, you can guess the rest. Teachers had forgotten details about the system. Few knew how to work their way out of problems. And remember that their button punching and muttered cursing was taking place while they were trying to look after lively tutor groups in an urban comprehensive school.

As a result, when I visited, I found that a senior deputy head had turned into a full-time trouble shooter, along with the almost permanently resident whiz-kid from the software company. And, crucially and unsurprisingly, the staff had turned against it all. They just didn't want to know about the advantages. They just wanted their big friendly paper registers back.

You can argue that the problem lay in the speed of innovation. There's more to it than that, though. Had everyone been convinced that this was the right way to go, and that it would quickly change their lives for the better, they'd have plunged cheerfully in amid a welter of black humour and improvised tricks. How else has the electronic whiteboard – so obviously the teacher's friend – become almost a universal classroom tool in a very short time?

No, it was more than that. The fundamental error was to forget that this change, although imposed on everyone, seemed intended mainly to help management and administration. The primary purpose of electronic registration is to make it easier – much, much easier – for management to handle and analyse the school's attendance data. There are benefits for teachers working with groups in the classroom, but they're not so obvious, and they emerge more slowly. If you're not careful, then, as in the case I've described, people at the sharp end start with nothing but extra work and the loss of familiar routines – yet more problems dumped from above.

The good news is that nobody would do it like that now. Schools have had to learn how to innovate. They know now to go slowly, to pilot new ideas with willing volunteers across limited cohorts, and to keep in touch with other schools, especially those that are finding the oil on the track.

Just a thought to cheer you, though, if you're an eager pioneer. Masten Gregory was a favourite of David Letterman, the US talk show host. Once, having described him, Letterman summed up why he envied him: 'Well, there you go. That's the complete picture, isn't it? He was a daredevil, living in Paris and a ladies' man.' On balance, once upon a time, I'd have happily put up with a bit of oil on the track to be a daredevil ladies' man living in Paris. Not now though.

Delegation's not just letting go

Delegation is a necessary part of leadership. But it's not at all the same as 'letting go' and abdicating responsibility. I once had dinner with the principal of a large FE college. He told me that when he took over the job, he'd listed his responsibilities, then taken a rule and divided the list into four. Then he'd handed each section over to one of his vice principals. I guess that was something of an exaggeration, but I certainly got the idea. And yet, no one at any time could say that he wasn't in charge of the college. There was no misunderstanding about that.

'I'm in charge'

Bruce Forsyth, national treasure and multi-talented host of the BBC's *Strictly Come Dancing* TV show, started compèring ITV's *Sunday Night at the London Palladium* in 1958. His mock-desperate cry of 'I'm in charge!' soon became the catchphrase of national choice and a career-long fixture for Bruce.

It resonates so well because everyone in any sort of working environment is familiar with the spectacle of the panic-stricken supervisor or manager suddenly realising that the whole caboodle is slipping out of control, going downhill and shedding bits as it goes, like that big cannon in Stanley Kramer's *The Pride and the Passion*. (Now there's another leadership parable I should return to.)

It's easy to see how it happens. The leader allows the team to get on with the job, either because that's what you're supposed to do, or out of simple laziness, and then realises, too late, that it's all going wrong. In the world of finance, it's Barings Bank suddenly realising that Nick Leeson has left them with a loss of £827 million. In school it's the head's realisation that one department is about to blow a hole in the year's

GCSE results. In cases like that, Bruce's cry of 'I'm in charge!' becomes more of a confession than an assertion of authority.

The trick, clearly, is to get the balance right between letting people do their thing on the one hand, while on the other hand making sure that they do it in full knowledge of where the boundaries lie.

What's surely true, for example, is that the clear 'I'm in charge' statement has to come at the beginning of any enterprise, not when things are fraying at the edges. That seems easy enough, but how does it chime with the notion that you need to listen, hang back and provide space?

One of the best demonstrations of how it to do it was by Louis V. Gerstner Jr, who rescued IBM from near bankruptcy in the early nineties. In his account of those years (*Who Says Elephants Can't Dance?*), he describes how, very early in his appointment, attending a review of one of the IBM businesses, he found himself expected to sit through a lecture by the manager, illustrated with OHP transparencies or 'foils'.

'Nick was on his second foil,' writes Gerstner, 'when I stepped to the table and, as politely as I could in front of his team, switched off the projector. After a long moment of awkward silence, I simply said, "Let's just talk about your business".'

Within a day, Gerstner's action in hitting the off button was a talking point across IBM's 300,000 people worldwide. Nothing could have said more clearly both 'I'm in charge!' and 'I'm ready to listen to you.'

(For me the bravest bit of this was Gertner's assumption that he'd be able to find the switch on the projector first time. I'd have spoiled the whole thing by having to ask where it was.)

Gerstner, clearly, didn't want to be shown diagrams of what was wrong, or right, about one branch of his empire. He was the leader, not the manager of detail.

'I manage by principle, not procedure,' he said. Part of that meant that he didn't want people running to him with their problems.

'Solve problems laterally,' he told his managers. 'Don't keep bringing them up the line.'

Can we distil some points for school leaders from this?

Doing the 'I'm in charge' thing early on is an obvious one. IBM was in big trouble when Gerstner arrived and he quickly took some drastic steps, but it was the OHP incident that became what his book calls 'the click heard round the world'. The equivalent in school might be dropping a regular meeting that often has nothing to talk about, or getting the caretaker to erase the word 'Head' on a parking space. ('If I'm not here in time to get a space, I'll take my chances.') All are actions where the symbolism is more important than the message.

The instruction to 'solve problems laterally' is worth thinking about, too. The opposite – allowing 'upward delegation' – can put the leader in a difficult position. I've told the story before – it had such a strong effect on me – of how I once tried to involve a senior education officer in a difficult decision and how he was having none of it, saying, in an entirely friendly way, 'Tackle it, Gerald. Then let me know.'

It's a phrase I recommend. Use it soon. Look your worried colleague in the eye and say, 'Tackle it. Then let me know.'

The Pride and the Passion (1957) Dir. Stanley Kramer. Starring Cary Grant, Frank Sinatra and Sophia Loren.
Lois V. Gerstner Jr (2002) *Who Says Elephants Can't Dance? Inside IBM's Historic Turnaround*, London: Harper Collins.

Slow but sure

There's no 'quick fix' for a school in trouble, no matter how much we – or more precisely the government of the day – wish there were. At international level, there can hardly be a better example of a problem that could never, at any time, have been quickly solved than that of what to do about the Middle East.

In the desert, you can't hurry

T.E. Lawrence, 'Lawrence of Arabia' (1888–1935), really was that cliché, 'a legend in his own lifetime'. Not only that, but the West's continuing involvement in the Middle East constantly brings him to mind, which is presumably why at one point the Pentagon circulated its generals with some of Lawrence's sayings, including: 'War upon rebellion is messy and slow, like eating soup with a knife.'

When I read that one, I couldn't help thinking that it could apply quite well to the business of school improvement. Rather than being passed down from above, though, it could be used by the schools themselves as a reminder to a government which appears at times to think that a school can be quickly turned round by changing its name and status. The truth, though, is that deep-rooted change in a stressed and complicated organisation – the Arab nations of 1918 or a twenty-first-century school – takes longer than you think.

Part of the problem is that any leader involved in making changes understandably likes to announce good news as early as possible. There's pressure, and the accountability, and a political need to demonstrate progress.

To this end, of course, leaders often do something very visible right at the start, so a head teacher, for example, will do some cosmetics, such as tightening up on uniform, improving the entrance hall, putting up a new school sign at the gate.

Ask the right questions, though, and you start to learn the things they'll only tell you off the record – of the long, slow business, for example, of lifting the spirits of down and demoralised staff. That alone is energy-sapping, and it explains why moving into a failing school requires some very special qualities of resilience. Without them, the new head can be dragged down rather than the staff pulled upward.

That's not the only or even the biggest problem though. Most schools that have had a long period of decline have within them some staff – teachers and others – who aren't going to be won over and who, in the end, have to go. Some will depart of their own accord. A few will be levered out on the promise of retirement deals (rarer now than they used to be). In the end, though, there's almost bound to be some who will simply need to be sacked.

Now that is no easy matter. You don't just go up to anyone, in any walk of life, these days and say, 'You're fired!' What you do is start a 'procedure', and it's, yes, 'messy and slow, like eating soup with a knife'. Most people employed in schools are, rightly, supported by unions. And, again rightly, these unions are very careful to ensure that their members are fairly treated. Ask any head who's succeeded in dismissing a member of staff what the process was like and you'll get the story of a fraught, insomnia-inducing time that he or she would just as soon forget.

Many of Lawrence's frustrations of later life – when he sought anonymity in the ranks first of the army and then, until the end of his life, the RAF – were brought about by the frustrations of his 'hero' period. He'd poured his soul into an enterprise that, in the end, seemed to have been in vain. (The British government wasn't inclined to live up to Lawrence's vision of Arab self-determination – and we can see where that's left us.) He was lonely, too, beset by a feeling, I guess, that none of the people who praised his achievements really and truly understood what he'd gone through to make them happen.

Transforming heads must feel the same way. They'll take the pat on the arm from the chair of governors at the drinks gathering in the library. They may even give talks to other heads. But they'll never really be able to shake off the feeling that nobody really understands what it was truly like to have some of those fraught conversations, or to listen to bitter appeals from people in danger of losing their jobs, or to the careful forensic analysis of a union rep who knows exactly what the rules are.

They won't have – as your family has – seen you staring into space over the dinner table at home, at a time when the comfortable familiarity of your previous job seemed both far away and very inviting.

It all calls for a rare blend of personal and professional leadership qualities. The trick, I suppose, is to concentrate on the positive, to be assured that the majority of people, defeated and doubtful though they may initially be, will rally to the cause, leaving only a small number who in the end will have to leave. Always there are many moments when it seems it'll never come right. One head I interviewed some years ago, who eventually wrought total transformation in a city school, went through intensely dark times, at one time having to be personally persuaded by the Chief Education Officer not to give it all up. Sanity survived, in his case, because without realising it he was faithful to another of the Pentagon's timeless Lawrence utterances: 'It is their war and you are to help them, not win it for them.'

Just tell them what to do

Dennis Hayes, a teacher educator, wrote in the TES *in May 2007: 'in this hypersensitive world you can't put across any ideas in a firm way, because any view held with conviction is seen as confrontational'.*

Benjamin Cheever, the rather less famous son of famous writer John Cheever, had clearly been accustomed to that world of evasion. As a result, when he went to work among people struggling to make a living, and found there wasn't time for pussyfooting around, he learned a lesson and found the experience refreshing.

The thoughts I try to express in this column cover only part of what I found to reflect on in Cheever's book and I recommend it. As is so often the case, it's more rewarding – and easier to read – than many a school management text.

Ben does his best

Benjamin Cheever, as a struggling writer, was forced at times to seek unskilled work around New York in order to make ends meet. His experiences eventually appeared as *Selling Ben Cheever*, which makes absorbing reading.

He did a range of very different jobs, including security guard, shop worker, fast-food server, but one thing they had in common was that they were invariably hedged around with a whole lot of rules. Everything was set down in writing. That's presumably because not many people stayed in the jobs for long, and so the job descriptions had to be set out clearly. It's also true to say that some recruits were operating, to put it kindly, at the outer limits of their abilities. If they'd had real initiative and judgement, they wouldn't be drifting around these jobs in the first place – at least that's clearly what the employers assumed. Rarely were these rules couched in intimidatory style. They just set out, in neutral terms, what was to be done. Sometimes the reasons were given – when Ben did a stint as Santa, for example, his duplicated list of rules included:

'Eating garlic prior to assuming your chimney post may drive down revenue for the day.'

'Keeping your suit and beard clean while on the streets is a good thing.'

And at other times, such as when he picked up the rules for being a security guard, there seemed no need to give any reasons.

'Turn off coffee machines. Do not turn off computers. Report burned-out lightbulbs. Express no opinion.'

When Cheever was actually doing these jobs, he invariably met the same level of clarity. Take, for example, one of Cheever's best jobs, which was behind the counter of a sandwich bar, building bespoke sandwiches for Manhattan customers in a hurry. He was slow and lacking dexterity, but he liked pleasing customers and he appreciated the way his co-workers – all much younger – treated him. Between them, they managed a combination of kindness and firm direction that any team with a new member might learn from.

'Halfway through my first day,' he writes, 'the manager put a hand on my waist and one on my shoulder. "Would you do me a big favour?" he asked. "Sure", I said. "Would you please not cut everybody's sandwich in half? If they ask you to cut it in half, then do that. But don't offer to cut everybody's sandwich in half. You're slowing the line."'

There was much about Cheever's life as a bottom-of-the pile worker that Cheever disliked – it would be absurdly romantic to pretend otherwise. What he did appreciate, though, was the clarity of the discourse.

'My co-workers weren't always friendly, but they were always present, always direct. There were squabbles but there seemed to be very little hypocrisy. I was part of a team here. I felt loyal, included.'

You've been a customer in places like that, haven't you? The staff are smiling, they're helping each other. As they cross in front of each other there's a joke and a friendly touch. A highly visible supervisor is unashamedly supervising. You watch and you detect what you suddenly realise is pride – that feeling of 'We're good at this. We can do it!'

That plain, unambiguous discourse is surely at the heart of it. It's called, I suppose, 'knowing where you stand'. You can't have a good, busy, positive team unless people can speak clearly to each other and – importantly – can accept what's said.

And it's that, I think, that we're not always good at in schools. Do we have 'squabbles but little hypocrisy'? I'm really not sure. We make great play of the importance of teamwork, but we can't easily achieve the direct parlance that's surely necessary to make it work. Without it – if people don't say what they mean, if they hold back for fear of offending – then sooner or later the team will fall apart.

That avoidance of directness is probably something to do with the role of the teacher – someone who instinctively tries to avoid confrontation. So the anger that's sparked off in a staff meeting gets played out somewhere else – at home, perhaps, following a slammed door.

'He's stark raving mad! It won't work!'
'I see. Did you tell him that?'
'Of course not, do you take me for a fool?'

When Ben Cheever left the sandwich bar, he took good memories away. He hoped it would thrive:

'The bread is good. It's fabulous. I hope they remember the second gimmick too, though. It's kindness.'

One final, rather sombre point. The people who research life in the low-pay zone all comment on how often they meet people who were once in good professional jobs – doctors, lawyers and, er, teachers. The fall of the professional from grace is more common than we think.

On the plus side, of course, is that most teachers have access to a Santa suit, and many, mostly senior leadership team members, have actual experience of the role. So the moral is, make sure you know, at all times, where your school's Santa suit is located so that, if necessary, you can pick it up as you hurry out of the door in disgrace.

Back to Square One In a Service Economy, Harrisonburg, USA.
Ben Cheever (2001) *Selling Ben Cheever*, London: Bloomsbury.

Dealing with the maverick team member

We all know about the brilliant team member who doesn't play by the rules. Sometimes the leadership is tolerant of a person like that, believing that it's just what the team needs, and that anyway it's results that count. But when the maverick's contemporaries and subordinates start to say, with increasing emphasis, that things have gone too far, then maybe it's time for those in authority to take another look at what's going on. This story is a classic illustration of what can go wrong when a highly able but anarchic middle leader is given too much rope. It's much quoted in management circles for that reason.

Listen to the people who know

We all know about the maverick team member – the one who only obeys the rules when they're convenient, and who then relies for approval on a combination of chutzpah and on-the-job flair. We've worked with people like that, and endured seeing them indulged by an apparently myopic leadership.

For a really stark example of the maverick's influence and ultimate fate, though, we should look at the case of Lieutenant-Colonel Arthur 'Bud' Holland of the United States Air Force.

From 1971 into the mid-nineties, Bud Holland flew B-52 bombers – those monsters with eight jet engines that we've seen in news footage dropping bombs from the stratosphere on a range of countries from Vietnam to Iraq. An immensely skilled pilot, he flew the big beast like a fighter plane – high-speed runs just above the ground, tight turns, steep climbs. He broke the rules all the time – too low, too fast, too steep. And just to underline the point, he always parked his car in a prohibited zone on the base. And what did higher authorities do? They shook their heads indulgently and said, 'Well, that's old Bud for you!'

So have you known someone like that? Turning up late for lessons, missing meetings, undermining other people's discipline and all the time getting away with it on the strength of long service and on-the-job brilliance?

If so, remember two things about Bud Holland.

First, that although the commanders above him were unfailingly complimentary – 'Bud is as good a B-52 aviator as I have seen', says one official report – closer colleagues told a different story.

'I'm not going to fly with him', said one. 'He's going to kill somebody some day and it's not going to be me.'

Second, and most importantly, Bud Holland's confidence eventually and inevitably outran his abilities. In June 1994, attempting a steep turn close to the ground at his own base, he crashed his B-52 killing himself and his crew in front of his own family.

(Incidentally, if you think that the person who said, 'He's going to kill somebody one day', was being uncannily prophetic, then think again. The truth is that lots of people were saying it, and pleading with higher authority to do something. There were many recorded incidents of Bud Holland's recklessness. On one occasion he flew so close to a hilltop that his co-pilot intervened on the controls. The final accident was clearly foreseeable and therefore preventable.)

Since it happened, the Bud Holland tragedy has generated endless debate in the military and beyond about the leadership failings that led up to it. (Major Kern's paper, reference below, is a good example.)

What emerges is that Colonel Holland thrived in a culture where top management excused or ignored out-of-control behaviour partly from fear of seeming to stifle initiative and partly from straightforward distaste for confrontation. Major Kern calls it 'an unhealthy state of apathy and non-compliance'.

A sure sign that much was wrong in Holland's unit was that lower ranking colleagues became disillusioned with senior leaders who, by tolerating Holland's behaviour, were putting crew members in harm's way. At least one officer left the service as a result. Some feigned illness to avoid working with Holland. One actually pretended to be ill while in the air, in order to make him settle down and behave himself.

Perhaps even more worrying was a tendency for some less experienced B-52 pilots to assume that they, too, could misbehave while in charge of a bomber with a fully loaded weight of 200 tonnes, flying over populated areas. One, for example, was reprimanded after climbing his aircraft nearly vertically until the speed dropped to about 75 mph, at which point it wasn't really flying at all.

All in all, the atmosphere was something like the grumbling, risk-taking staffroom anarchy that you sometimes find in an inadequately led school. Of course, in school, loose-cannon behaviour doesn't lead to tragedy. (Though the reports on some school trip incidents might tell us otherwise.) Effects on children's learning, though, and on teachers' careers, are real and long-lasting.

Colonel Holland was as much a victim as anyone of course. Good leadership would have reined him in and built on his abilities – and saved his life. There were many occasions when his superiors could, and should, have grasped the validity of the feelings of people lower down. Major Kern recognises this clearly. The point he makes – and it's valid in all settings, including schools – is that any leader may be faced with a problem that's been identified not by him but to him by the organisation as a whole.

We've all been there, haven't we? Trusted colleagues – a deputy maybe, or two or three heads of department – put their fingers on a weak spot and come to the leadership with it. Does the leader trust their judgement? Or does he or she become defensive and tell everyone to calm down and stop worrying? Or is the response – and this is very common – something like: 'Yes, yes, I'll deal with it in due course'?

Leadership, clearly, isn't all sweetness and light. Sometimes it's necessary to face down Mr Charisma. But the interesting thing is that once the deed is done, the nettle grasped, the first thing you hear is a widespread murmur of approval.

Major Tony Kern, USAF (1995) *Darker Shades of Blue: A Case Study of Failed Leadership.* Available online at www.crm-devel.org/resources/paper/darkblue/darkblue.htm

Epiphany moments

Teaching in general, and headship in particular, creates some wonderful moments. Sometimes these just live in the memory, bringing a smile to the lips when they surface. Occasionally, though, it's more than that, and a single moment is seen as somehow defining, life-changing even.

Moondust

Over a period of three wondrous years, between July 1969 and December 1972, twelve men – astronauts of NASA's epic Apollo missions – walked on the moon. Nine of them are still alive at the time of writing, and thirty years on author Andrew Smith set out to interview them all, curious to discover how they now felt about what they did then. The result is his absorbing book *Moondust*.

All nine of the moon walkers, he finds, were changed by the experience, and found frustrations in their lives afterwards. Buzz Aldrin of Apollo 11, now active as a promoter of space exploration, was for years a depressive alcoholic. Al Bean, of Apollo 12, endlessly paints moon scenes – nothing else – trying to portray and preserve not just what he saw but how he felt. Gene Cernan, of Apollo 17 – the last man on the moon – says, simply and tellingly: 'It's kind of tough to find an encore.'

It's Edgar Mitchell, of Apollo 14, who sums up their common feeling. Out there he had what he calls his 'epiphany' and wrote afterwards: 'The view from space has shown me – as no other event in my life has – how limited a view man has of his own life and that of the planet.'

It occurred to me as I read about these men – and the quality of Smith's writing is such that you do engage with them – that becoming a head teacher, in charge of a school, responsible for young lives and adult careers, is in its own way a life-changing rocket ride into a dangerous space. There are frustrations – and, as we know, there are casualties.

I chatted recently about all of this – the highs and lows of leading an urban comprehensive – with Sir Robert Dowling, honoured for the transformations he's wrought at George Dixon International School which serves a diverse and demanding community in Birmingham. He was eloquent – and colourfully funny – on the external pressures from government and critics, but about the burden of the core mission he was deadly serious.

'It's the enormity of the responsibility for the children that weighs on you', he says. 'The knowledge that you are the only chance they have – trying to get them to see that they really can have the same opportunities as Prince Harry.'

Sir Robert took on George Dixon in 1999, having already worked wonders at a Birmingham special school, and it's reasonable to assume that one of the keys to school improvement nationally lies in the willingness of able heads to move on to other challenges. The pressures of headship, though, are increasing – the government threatens to close poor schools that aren't quickly turned round. Why, then, should a successful head take on another school if the demands are going to be greater than they were the first time round? Kay Askew, the Principal of the North Liverpool Academy, believes that this is one reason behind the current dearth of headship applications.

'When you've reached a career high, you're reluctant to leave it and take on a new challenge', she says.

Fortunately, there are still some, Kay Askew included, who do move on. Why, I wondered, did she take the plunge? Her answer offers a clue that might be picked up by governing bodies looking to make headship appointments.

'It was when I met the children', she says. 'I asked them what they wanted from a new head, and they came up with what seem like simple things – a football team, a choir – bits of school life that you normally take for granted. Then one of them asked, 'Could we do a show?' I was won over. How could I walk away from them?'

For heads and teachers who are pressured and looking into darkness, it's always a meeting with children that becomes the equivalent of Astronaut Ed Mitchell's epiphany moment. Sir Robert actually used the word.

'I'll tell you about my epiphany', he said. 'It was five-thirty in the evening, and I was chatting to a cleaner, when thirty or so kids came walking across the hall. I asked them where they'd been, and they said they'd stayed behind for extra English and maths. They gathered round, some sat on the floor, and we just chatted about their hopes and aspirations. I thought to myself, "By Jesus, we're getting something right! These kids are buying into the message!"

Andrew Smith (2005) *Moondust: In Search of the Man Who Fell to Earth*, London: Bloomsbury.

Think about the impression you're making

Leaders influence their people in all manner of subtle ways, even when they're not aware of it. Body language, a casual word, can be enough to start a rumour running. The effect is much worse at a time of crisis or pressure, and it's something that leaders need to be aware of.

Fix your face before you go out

One of the things leaders at every level quickly learn and frequently forget is that when there's pressure on from outside, and everyone's worried, the boss's every word, action, gesture, even facial expression is scrutinised for mood and meaning. The commander of a helicopter squadron on one of the carriers en route to liberate the Falklands in those spring days of 1982 describes how, twelve hours after he'd read a personal letter containing bad news, he realised that even though he'd said nothing to anyone about his problem, everyone had picked up on his preoccupied and rather sombre manner, and the whole mood of his squadron had changed. Immediately, he deliberately started walking around with a smile on his face, and sure enough, everyone cheered up again: 'I thought, "Good Lord, is this the level of responsibility I have for these guys?"'

The most obvious parallel for us – inadequate to the point of bathos though it may be – is how the leadership bears up during the brief run-up to an inspection by Ofsted or the local authority. Too many heads have committed the almost unforgiveable sin of transmitting their own panic to the staff – nervily asking for documents, parading round looking at wall displays, holding unscheduled meetings, rushing past people without speaking.

Some time ago, I interviewed a number of heads about their approach to an impending Ofsted. One of them told me, in emotional terms, how badly he felt about having allowed his own worries to leak out to the staff.

'I'll regret that for the rest of my career', he said.

Others spoke of the almost physically painful effort to remain outwardly calm, cheerful and encouraging.

'I'd come out of my room and before going any further I'd quite deliberately stand still for a moment to relax and get the worry out of my face', said one.

But perhaps the best example of how to transmit optimism comes from that same Falklands operation. One evening, J.J. Black, Captain of HMS *Invincible*, having been told that some of his people were understandably worried and despondent, spoke to the ship's company over the internal TV system. After the usual encouraging words, he finished, quite spontaneously, with: 'quite frankly, I think we'll piss it. Good night.'

As soon as he emerged from giving his broadcast, sailors were stopping him to echo his words, and almost within minutes, there were home-made posters around the ship, and T-shirts, with the words 'We'll piss it with J.J.'.

What would any leader, anywhere, give for that level of trust and loyalty?

Hugh McManners, *Forgotten Voices of the Falklands*, London: Ebury Press.

Things to do

When the going gets tough, the tough make lists of things to do. Making a list, after all, provides a comforting sense that you've actually taken action. And seeing that huge and impenetrable cloud of competing demands reduced to a few words on an A4 sheet somehow seems to reduce your blood pressure all on its own.

A little list

Sir Christopher Bland, chairman of BT, is reputedly famous for keeping lists of Things to Do. That's quite a comfort to the rest of us, because we tend to think of list-making as a bit of a weakness – Sir Christopher himself described it in an interview once as 'a serious character flaw'.

In my experience, lists are what you turn to when there's so much to do that you're starting to hyperventilate. There's a feeling of relief as what was an inchoate mass of responsibilities and tasks magically condenses out into clearly defined bullet points. 'Revise School Improvement Plan', 'Advertise for new caretaker', 'Ask ICT manager what "bandwidth" means.'

And, the one that appears on everyone's list: 'Book car in for service (N.B. "ching-ching" noise when turning left)'.

One of my college friends made 'to do' lists all the time. He found that he could compose them while simultaneously playing the saxophone, the worse for drink, in his underpants. (This recalled image kept us comfortably amused whenever, in later years, we observed him in his pomp as principal of a large higher education establishment.)

There's some interesting research on 'to do' lists in Chuck Martin's book *Tough Management*. 'Most lists', he writes, 'have six to ten items, although it's daunting to learn that six percent of lists have more than forty.'

He's also looked into how well the tasks are completed. Most people, it seems, get somewhere between a third and two-thirds of their daily jobs done and, entirely predictably, just one person in a hundred manages the whole lot. It's mildly entertaining to reflect on what kind of person that one in a hundred is. And we all have a good idea, don't we?

Martin includes some pithy quotes from practitioners on their use of lists. So on the one hand there's the person who finds that the job changes so much it's hardly worth making a list at all, and on the other there's the manager who uses the list as a low-key entry to the day: 'I generally start by completing an easy item before trying to tackle the top priority.'

(That's the exact opposite of the conventional advice, which is to plunge into difficult things straight away and not indulge in displacement activity by doing something easy.)

I reckon, though, that many school leaders will be on the side of the one who writes, 'The number of incoming items and areas requiring vigilant monitoring continues to replace if not outpace the speed at which items can be considered complete.' (I have to say, though, that if it takes this guy twenty-five words to say: 'I've got too much to do', no wonder he's in trouble.)

None of Martin's subjects, though, seem to emulate Sir Christopher's alleged habit of adding items to his lists that he's already done, just to have the satisfaction of ticking them off. Now that is seriously worrying. I wonder if he plays the sax?

Chuck Martin (2005) *Tough Management: The 7 Ways to make Tough Decisions Easier, Deliver the Numbers, and Grow Business in Good Times and Bad*, New York: McGraw-Hill.

Small beginnings

Can huge movements trace their origins to a single event? We like to think so – we've all learned about the assassination of the Archduke Franz Ferdinand. So, although the truth is undoubtedly more complicated, I speculate in this column on the idea that the massive upheaval that's gone through the UK school system in the last thirty years was sparked off by a small group of teachers in a single London school.

The butterfly flaps her wings

Somewhere in this big world of ours, a butterfly is fluttering her wings. As a consequence, at some point in the future, something big will happen – I don't know, maybe America will invade Belgium.

Edward Lorenz's 'butterfly theory' is an attractive one. Did you ever wonder, for example, just how we got to where we are, in a highly regulated regime with a National Curriculum, prescribed lessons and the most comprehensively tested children in the world? Where's the butterfly flap that brought us here?

One candidate, for me, is found in the pages of the Auld Report which appeared in 1976. Commissioned by the Inner London Education Authority, the report arose from an investigation by Robin Auld QC into 'the teaching, organisation and management of the William Tyndale Junior and Infant Schools, Islington'.

What became known as 'the William Tyndale affair' began in January 1974 with the appointment of Terry Ellis as head of the junior school.

Mr Ellis, with deputy Brian Haddow, a strong-minded and able teacher with radical views, was soon running a highly progressive team-teaching regime that gave children a great deal of choice and freedom. It was essentially a system, much debated at the time, called 'the integrated day', where children chose their learning activities and there was no imposed timetable and no visible distinction between subjects. It was fashionable for a while – Leicestershire primaries pioneered it – but it was clear to many even at the time that while it could be made to work well with gifted teachers and good leadership, in less certain hands it could just as well be a recipe for chaos.

The result is described in the excellent *William Tyndale: Collapse of a School – or a System?* by *TES* journalists Mark Jackson and John Gretton, published with admirable speed by Allen & Unwin in 1976 as a *TES* special.

'No place in the school was put out of bounds to them [the pupils], not even the staff commonroom and lavatories', write Jackson and Gretton. 'They were allowed to eat sweets whenever they wanted, wherever they wanted. To all intents and purposes there were no rules at all.'

It was one of a number of bold experiments that went on at that time. Already it was clear that traditional methods of schooling weren't particularly effective, and many people were ready to try something else. So we had, for example, some 'free schools', and in Leicestershire a new kind of comprehensive in Countesthorpe. Common to all of them was a conviction on the part of their founders that compulsion, coercion and authoritarian denial of choice all added up to a dead end, particularly for those working-class children who had neither the resources nor the social resilience to make the best of what they were given.

The problem was that we just weren't ready for that degree of freedom. Society – particularly the media – was deeply suspicious, and teachers weren't trained or equipped for it. All of the progressive schools at that time became the focus of criticism from the media and often also from the local community. The difference with Tyndale, though, was the degree to which the school's internal dissent and conflict became luridly public. Those Tyndale teachers who didn't agree with what was happening made their views known – in one case by making common cause with disgruntled parents, fomenting discontent in a way that even the Auld Report called 'disgraceful'. Parents, for their part, voted with their feet and the roll plummeted. The press had a field day ('the school of shame') and the authority, in the absence of any clarity about its role in the management and teaching within its schools, ran round in circles wringing its collective hands.

It's impossible to resist the conclusion that it was all down to a failure of leadership either within the school or the authority, or both, on a scale that just wouldn't be allowed to develop now. For one thing, today's schools face up to performance criteria that simply didn't exist in the seventies.

'It is difficult to talk of assessing the performance of teachers when there is no agreement on what teachers are supposed to be doing', wrote Jackson and Gretton in 1976.

They conclude that the answer lay with the government – only it could bring the local authorities to heel and set some rules for judging schools.

'After William Tyndale, the Secretary of State can no longer pretend, as he and his predecessors have so often tended to do, that it is all happening somewhere else', they write.

So, for good or ill, the government sat up and began to take a grip. In October 1976, hard on the heels of the Tyndale business, Prime Minister James Callaghan made his keynote Ruskin College speech, raising doubts about what he described as 'the new informal methods of teaching, which seem to produce excellent results when they are in well-qualified hands but are much more dubious when they are not'.

So it was that painfully but irresistibly we edged towards the Education Reform Act of 1988, the National Curriculum, assessment, and all that's followed.

You can read the message of the Tyndale butterfly in various ways. Perhaps it was a much-needed catalyst for the restoration of order from imminent chaos, and the development of a strong framework within which leadership could operate. Or, on the other hand, maybe those teachers, by taking too radical an approach to freedom and choice, opened the door to the new authoritarians and in doing so set back, perhaps permanently, any prospect of a truly progressive approach to teaching in our primary schools. What do you think?

Mark Jackson and John Gretton (1976) *William Tyndale: Collapse of a School – or a System?*, London: Allen & Unwin.

Don't interfere when they know what they're doing

A school is one of those organisations (I guess the police force is another) in which the top people have come up, seamlessly, from the sharp end. A head still claims to be teacher, and is proud of being able (in theory that is) to walk into any classroom and take over.

That's good, of course. Maybe, though, it's one reason why people in the middle – phase and subject leaders – can find it difficult to exercise their leadership, constrained as they are by the looming presence of those at the top.

There are some organisations, though, where departments are doing widely different jobs, few of which the top person could tackle. When it's like that, the leadership has no option but to leave the department heads in complete charge. Can we learn from them?

Just let me get on with it

There's one bit of cruise ship tradition I always enjoy. It's when the captain, on the first formal evening, introduces his heads of department. We are told each person's area of responsibility, name and country of origin (cheers from varying parts of the room) and it's always done with generosity, obvious pride and laconic good humour. What strikes you, though, is how disparate are these people's responsibilities. There's maybe six or eight of them, including an engineer, a financial expert, a housekeeper, a bar manager and, of course, the head chef, in a tall hat (biggest cheer of all). The captain is in charge of them all, yet because he obviously can't engage with the details (what does he know of cocktail mixing, managing the bed linen, or making a thousand baked Alaskas?), each department head has no option but to be the one who clearly and visibly holds his or her team very much to account. The captain, of course, has many ways of knowing the level of efficiency of each department, but there's no doubt that the department head is the one responsible for the performance of individuals.

I thought about this when I read *Getting Out Through the Middle*, a study from the National College for School Leadership of five schools working their way out of failing Ofsted categories, and in particular of the role played by middle leaders.

Setting the background, the study points out that despite the acknowledged importance of middle leaders to school improvement, there's plenty of evidence nationally of subject leaders' reluctance to take on the task of leading and improving classroom practice in their areas. They've seen themselves rather as 'subject administrators', the assumption being that the monitoring of classroom practice is the job of the head and deputy.

In these five failing schools, therefore, the key to success lay in a determined and ultimately successful effort, carried out in various ways by the five heads, to change that – to help heads of department become effective middle leaders. In at least one school, the symbolic title change of 'subject manager' to 'middle leader' was made at the outset.

It wasn't always an easy business. When you think about it, it can be seen as transforming someone who is *primus inter pares* – more a colleague than a boss, perhaps even an ally in the battle against authority – into a more distant establishment figure.

However, one way or another, the middle leaders in these schools were persuaded and trained, sometimes with outside consultancy help, to take on the responsibility. They became key figures in monitoring the quality of teaching and learning in providing support for improvement. And, in the end, the progress that each of the schools made couldn't have been made had this particular challenge not been accepted at the start. The importance of this process is summed up by one of the heads: 'Could I have done it without the middle leaders? No, I don't think so. I needed them to preach the message. They are the missionaries out there selling it to their teams.'

Jenny Francis (2007) *Getting Out Through the Middle: The Role of Middle Leaders in the Journey from Failure to Success*. Available online at ncsl.org.uk/media/4EF/4E/Getting-out-through-the-middle-summary.pdf

Be open to bad news

In another article in this collection, I describe the 'Scheisskopf effect'. I named it after a character in Catch 22 *who insists on frankness from subordinates but in reality is likely to bite off the head of anyone bearing bad news.*

The effect is to stifle not just criticism but helpful advice. Too fearsome a leader risks not hearing timely warnings.

The story here picks up on the same theme, but this one's far from fictional. It's a very true and terrible illustration of one of the most fundamental errors of leadership.

Dare we tell him?

On 22 June 1893 eleven ships of the Royal Navy's Mediterranean Fleet were on manoeuvres off Beirut, led by Admiral Sir George Tryon.

The admiral had been in post for two years, and during that time he'd set out to shake things up. In particular, and with tragic irony given what was to happen, he was keen to develop a more questioning, independent attitude among junior officers.

In fact, though, such was the force of his personality and so strong were his reputation and record, that he had the opposite effect. Officers of the fleet felt intimidated and became even less likely to question him.

So it was that one June day, Tryon led his fleet to disaster, never seriously challenged by the many people, including senior captains, who saw it coming.

The fleet was steaming in two parallel lines – one of six ships, one of five – when Tryon gave the order for them all to reverse course and steam the opposite way. The leading two ships were to begin the course change by turning inwards towards each other. The other ships would follow. He clearly planned that the two lines would then be going the opposite way, but much closer together.

The trouble was, the starting distance between the two lines was six cables – 1200 yards – whereas everyone with any experience knew that at least eight cables – 1600 yards – would be needed to ensure that the lead ships didn't meet as they turned in towards each other. One senior officer questioned Tryon's order, suggesting that the lines move to eight cables apart. He got a flea in his ear for his pains and a piece of paper from Tryon with the number '6' written on it.

The die was cast. The leading ships, *Victoria* and *Camperdown* turned inwards on what was clearly a collision course. But as Captain Bourke of the *Victoria* later said in evidence: 'Open criticism of one's superior is not consonant with true discipline.'

At the last moment, Tryon agreed that *Victoria* should reverse her engines, but it was too late, and the ships crashed together. *Victoria*, ripped open, quickly sank and 357 men drowned, including Tryon himself, who made no effort to save himself. The disaster happened because subordinates – senior, seasoned leaders themselves – could not bring themselves to challenge their chief in anything but the most tentative way.

The phenomenon of the unchallenged leadership error is as problematic in schools as it is in any other walk of life. It can involve no more than an irritation. Imagine the head who calls an unscheduled meeting that inconveniences twenty people and causes the cancellation of rehearsals and team practices. Will someone say, politely but assertively: 'I really wish you'd think about this. Is it really necessary?'?

Or it can be more serious than that – a curriculum change made arbitrarily without proper consideration of the knock-on effects throughout the timetable, the use of the building and the feelings of parents.

What happens in these cases, all too often, is that people mutter but don't speak out. There was plenty of evidence of such muttering at the inquiry following Admiral Tryon's collision. Down the line of command, lots of questioning went on, and Tryon's second in command, in the ship opposite to Tryon's, went so far as to signal that he didn't understand the order, only to be told to shut up and get on with it. Which is what he did, even though it was his ship that collided with Tryon's. It takes real courage to challenge a decision made by someone who's risen to the top job and is assumed to be infallible.

And there lies another, very recognisable ingredient in this debacle. Tryon was not regarded as a fool – quite the opposite in fact. He came with a formidable reputation. Several of Tryon's subordinates said that they assumed the admiral knew something that they didn't.

And the answer? In good schools we have distributed leadership now, and a deliberate effort to release talent and leadership throughout the organisation. The autocratic head, handing down orders from above, may still exist, but is certainly in a minority, isolated from the mainstream, potentially a tragic figure like Admiral Sir George Tryon RN.

Don't assume the other person's job is better

Arguably the most enthralling documentary series of all time is ITV's Up *films, which began in 1964 with* Seven Up, *an account of the lives of fourteen British seven-year-olds from a range of socio-economic backgrounds. That film was fascinating in itself, but what turns it into pure gold is the director Michael Apted's return to the group every seven years to make an update. Each time he has persuaded a significant number of the originals to take part. At the time of writing the latest is 49* Up, *screened in 2005. The next,* 56 Up *will be out in late 2011 or early 2012.*

It may be greener, but it's still grass

Remember Bruce Balden? OK, let me add a few more names – Tony, Jackie, Symon, Andrew, Sue, Neil. That's right. It's that Bruce, from *49 Up*, the seventh in the award-winning series of TV documentaries that's followed a group of young people through their lives, starting in 1964 when they were seven, and the programme was *7 Up*.

Bruce was an idealist, highly educated. At forty-two – in *42 Up* – he had chosen to exercise his skills in an inner-city comprehensive. At forty-nine, though, we found him in a rather different place – a posh fee-paying school in fact. There he was, wearing a gown, singing in chapel, and looking frankly fabulous, every inch the part, like a character in a Terence Rattigan play.

I mention him because his move, and the evidence of what it had done for him, brought to life what for many teachers is a recurring dream – that perhaps, having laboured in the heat and dust, they might, in maturity, now reward themselves with less demanding jobs in another sort of school. A secondary teacher might fancy a primary class for example, or a primary teacher might think it would be easier just to teach one subject all the time in secondary, or either of them might think of joining Bruce in the private sector. Be assured they're normal feelings. You can read them on the *TES* website's 'staffroom' forum, and we've all been there.

It's the very familiar 'grass is greener' scenario, isn't it? And because using the term brings some negative vibes into play, it needs looking at in more detail. Why, for example, might a secondary school teacher want to move to a primary school? Ask the question of somebody who's attempting to do it and you'll hear various explanations – a broader curriculum, closer contact with one group of children ('my class'), the satisfaction of seeing young children make great strides with the basics. All of those are valid. Often, though, the real and honest reason is to do with discipline. Teaching in a secondary school these days is hard work. And in some schools it's more than that – it's actually a losing and debilitating battle against disaffection, brutality and open contempt for the values you hold dear. When it's like that, the prospect of working with keen youngsters who still want to learn and to please you starts to look like a career-saving, perhaps even a life-saving, option. There's a belief among many secondary school teachers that in the primary sector life is easier, gentler and more civilised.

Is it really like that? It can be. Some teachers make the move and never look back. Others, though, find that the skills of keeping order – of motivating children, winning them over – don't differ all that much between sectors. In other words, the bald truth is that if you're a poor disciplinarian in secondary, the chances are you'll still be one in primary. In many cases, for example, when you look at why a teacher is having trouble, it turns out to be largely a matter of organisation. The teacher who's not prepared for the lesson and has to fuss around looking for things, or inventing activities on the hoof, is creating opportunities for misbehaviour. In the primary sector, the need for good organisation is even greater. In fact the younger the children, the greater the need for a very high level of classroom organisation. Do you really think that the vague and unprepared secondary teacher is going to find life easy in a Reception class where an almost superhuman level of classroom management is called for?

Bruce Balden, of course, made a different sort of move – from an urban state secondary into the private sector. That, too, is something of a dream for some teachers. Many of the same cautions apply though. In fact it would be the gravest of mistakes to assume that someone who couldn't keep order in a comprehensive school classroom would find things easier in the private sector. The very opposite, in fact, might turn out to be the case. Moving across phases in any direction, in fact is no small undertaking. Anyone even thinking of making the leap needs to make visits, talk to heads, do some exchange teaching.

Bruce didn't leave the comprehensive because he couldn't hack it. On the contrary, by his own admission, he left because the continuous effort of successfully hacking it was wearing him down.

So whatever the nature of the siren call that's making you look at jobs in other sectors, the first priority is to be brutally honest with yourself about why you're unhappy where you are. Is it, in truth, because you've never actually been all that good at the job? Because if it is, then moving on won't help. If, for example, you aren't very good at discipline, then better, perhaps, to acknowledge and tackle your own issues, among friends and colleagues, with good professional support, before seeking the greener grass. There's never been a better time for this – one largely unsung effect of the current huge emphasis on school improvement has been to lift and rejuvenate the professionalism of many colleagues who've been underperforming for years.

Second, don't run away with the idea that Bruce's job is a sinecure. Every school and department has its own brand of pressure. No teaching job, taken seriously and done well, is easy and worry-free.

And third, if you've considered my first two points and are still bent on change, then go for it. Bruce, presumably, got his job after sending for a form and filling it in. That's the necessary starting point, and it's open to all.

If they don't get it, just tell them

Modern management theory espouses a more collaborative approach. In today's society, people are less willing to know their place, and accept just being told what to do. They require explanations, they need to have 'ownership' (a much used word) of decisions. Surely, though, there's a tension here? Isn't it sometimes necessary for a leader to use his or her authority and, in effect, give orders? Where's the borderline beween collaborative management and the wielding of authority? A good place to pin this down, I thought, would be in the armed forces, so I went to see somebody who's right at the top.

The Admiral has an 'F moment'

I talked to an admiral once, in his imposing Portsmouth residence. (I wasn't at all surprised to discover that Nelson had once lived there. The Royal Navy is like that.) I was asking him about the way that today's servicemen and women are encouraged to have initiative and to speak up about their tasks and duties. I wondered how this worked in a highly disciplined environment.

'Training and teamwork', he said. 'When there's an emergency, everyone knows what to do. If someone sees a way to solve a problem, they'll speak up.'

I was still a bit dubious.

'But surely', I said, 'there comes a moment when you have to say…'

Here he instantly interrupted. Thrusting his imposing head forward, he fixed me with his ocean-blue eyes and rapped out:

'Do as you're fucking told! Is that what you mean?'

'Er, yes. That would be it', I said, perceiving in that moment one reason why this genial and cultured man had become one of the most senior people in the whole of the UK armed forces.

Every since then, I've thought of the point at which the discussion has to be replaced by a direct instruction as the 'F moment'.

We don't have many flat-out 'F moments' in school leadership. We tend to say: 'Jack, would you mind looking after 10W after break?'

Or:

'Maggie, I wonder if you'd have a word with the caretaker and ask him if he'd mind talking to the cleaner in charge and asking her to see if the lady who does my room could have a go at the windows? Thank you ever so much.'

The problem with this approach is that when you do give a direct instruction, it's often interpreted as the beginning of a debate. A Warwickshire primary head recalled telling a young teacher not to park on the grass.

'He came up with reasons why he should park there', said the head. 'In the end I just had to look him in the eye and say: "You're making the mistake of thinking this is a discussion. It isn't."'

Mind you, even that approach can go wrong. A friend, a secondary deputy, told me gleefully of his head's attempt to get the caretaker to clean the fly-blown light fittings in the hall.

'Yes, I'll make a note ...'

'No. Do it now.'

'Right. As soon as I've ...'

'No. Get your ladder. Do it now.'

'Eventually,' said my friend, 'the caretaker stormed up his ladder in a temper, fell off it, and was on sick leave for six months.'

Leadership role models

Much play is made these days of 'management styles'. There is, for example, the authoritarian style that used to be favoured by head teachers, and is still found in some branches of business. I once met one of those 'old school' factory managers. I can recommend the experience, because it will convince you once and for all that frightening the people you work with is not a viable way to secure loyalty and improvement. Look instead to somebody like Ernest Shackleton who was well ahead of his time when it came to understanding the nature of true leadership.

Heading South

I spent a day once in a factory that made spare parts for cars. The manager there obviously thought I was a total wimp. When I asked about consultation with his staff, he looked at me as though I had offered him a year's free membership of the League of Marxist–Leninist Ballet Dancers.

'There are two ways of running any organisation', he boomed, zooming backwards on his swivel chair. 'You can pull it from the front, or drive it from behind. I prefer the second method.'

I have been trying to fathom the meaning of this ever since.

Was he a good leadership role model? Well, his people were clearly terrified of him – but at the same time, like the punters at Alton Towers, they quite liked being scared.

No, for me, the role model par excellence is Polar explorer Ernest Shackleton, who in 1916 brought all of his men home safely after a series of heartbreaking setbacks that included the loss of his ship and an 800-mile ocean crossing in a tiny lifeboat.

Known as 'the boss' throughout his career, Shackleton displayed qualities that, according to authors Margot Morrell and Stephanie Capparell, continue to inspire others. In *Shackleton's Way* they tell how

Michael Dale, president of Jaguar North America during the car importer's dark days, learned about optimism from Shackleton. 'He never gave the slightest sign, no matter how bad things got,' said Dale, 'that he wasn't going to survive.'

Shackleton was a very modern leader. His determination to pick the right team for the Antarctic led him to adopt a selection process we could all learn from. He wanted optimists, because they are likely to be good team players. He looked for hard workers who would take their share of the dirty jobs, and he wanted people who could do those tasks that he couldn't. Above all, of course, he needed the right deputy – resourceful, with a similar vision, and unfailingly loyal – and he found him in the superb Frank Wild.

To achieve the right mix, he asked applicants if they could sing, because he wanted people who would take part in morale-lifting evenings in the Antarctic winter. So when you look at Frank Hurley's expedition photographs, you're struck how many show the men enjoying themselves – all laughingly having their heads shaved on a whim, or toasting 'sweethearts and wives' after an evening meal. If you worked for Shackleton, you trusted him, and that made you comfortable enough to relax together.

Now isn't that how you'd like your school to be – a mixture of talents, each one given the opportunity to shine and to contribute to the common good? A few surprising and unexpected skills? The occasional spontaneous excursion into exuberant craziness? A wholly dependable deputy capable of holding things together in the face of adversity?

There are some staffrooms like that, just as there are miserable ones where people jump when the door opens in case it's the head.

My own leadership hero figure? I'm still looking, but I think there is a lot to be said for Master Sergeant Ernest Bilko of the classic fifties American TV comedy *Bilko* ('Trust me men, we're all going to be rich!'). He'd have won the South Pole in a poker game and presented it to a grateful nation – on a leaseback arrangement, of course.

Margot Morrell and Stephanie Capparell (2003) *Shackleton's Way: Leadership Lessons from the Great Antarctic Explorer*, London: Nicholas Brealey Publishing.

Leave room for the oddball

Teams are all very well in their place, but individuals are important too. It seems to me that the current trend towards producing teachers of uniform quality and style ignores the fact that a good school surely has room for people who work in ways other than those approved by agencies of the government. I remember an excellent maths teacher who would often address his classes while lying flat on the maths room window ledge. Ofsted, I have no doubt, would have frowned upon this, even though he did have a bad back.

In this column I started thinking about music hall performers of the past, some of whom were eccentric to the point where their audiences were so bewildered that there nothing else to do but laugh. Which is what it was all about I suppose.

A horse, walking

The great northern comic Frank Randle did part of his act sitting behind a drum kit. Suddenly, he would break off from his monologue and tap out a steady rhythm on the woodblocks.

'A horse, walking', he would announce, in a deliberately affected tone.

Then he would do it again, but with the sticks stopping just above the blocks so that there was only silence.

'A horse, walking in the snow', he would intone in the same faux posh voice. The audience would break up and he would cackle delightedly at the thought of once again getting away with such nonsense.

Can you imagine another comedian doing that? Jack Dee? Ricky Gervais? Of course not. And yet they're all effective at making people laugh. Suppose a busybody manager were to say to Jack Dee: 'Look, Jack, I've got this drum kit. I'd like you to sit behind it and do this. It worked for Frank Randle …'. And yet, aren't we in danger of doing that to our teachers when we fence them in with highly prescriptive strategies, lesson plans, schemes of work?

The danger of making everyone stick to guidelines – even 'proven' guidelines – is that you'll clip some people's wings and end up with mediocrity. It's a theme that Marcus Buckingham develops in his excellent book on management, *The One Thing You Need To Know* (Simon & Schuster). He takes as an example a successful retail store in which workers with special – sometimes quirky – individual skills are encouraged and directed to appropriate tasks. What you always hope for, he suggests, is that when someone challenges the orthodoxy coming from above, then those doing the handing down will stop and think about what they're asking: 'Thus challenged [leaders] will, or should, become more inquisitive, more intelligent, more vital, and more able to duck and weave into the future.'

Do you see that happening in education? Do ministers, education officers, inspectors, school leaders show signs of listening to creative people working at the sharp end, learning from them how to 'duck and weave into the future'?

No, neither do I. The hand of central direction rests heavily on the service at every level, making life for unorthodox and challenging teachers and heads more difficult than is good for the nation.

So, leader, whoever you are, look up from your desk for a moment today.

Cock your ear and listen for the sound of a horse walking in the snow.

Marcus Buckingham (2005) *The One Thing You Need to Know ... About Great Managing, Great Leading, and Sustained Individual Success*, London: Simon & Schuster.

Don't say 'tell me' unless you mean it

Someone once said that the most important attribute of a leader is the ability to fake sincerity. You have to take that with a pinch of salt, because fake sincerity has a way of betraying itself. In this piece I picked up on one of the characters in Catch 22, *an officer who insists that people come and tell when things are going wrong. Our hero, though, knows that it's not nearly as simple as that.*

Yossarian knew better

Head teachers – particularly, perhaps, those in primary schools, where teams are small and relationships close, depend heavily on colleagues keeping them in constant touch with emerging problems. Where this doesn't happen – where there's a feeling that people aren't being entirely frank with bad news – it may be because of what I call the 'Scheisskopf effect'.

Scheisskopf is the officer in Joseph Heller's *Catch 22* who insists that everyone be frank with him.

"'I want someone to tell me", Lieutenant Scheisskopf beseeched them all prayerfully. "If any of it is my fault, I want to be told."'

Yossarian's friend Clevinger takes him at his word.

"'He wants someone to tell him", Clevinger said. "He says he won't punish me."'

Yossarian, however, knows better.

"'He'll castrate you", said Yossarian.'

Scheisskopf knows that good management depends heavily on a good flow of information. Without it, problems can rumble and develop until they explode. At the same time, though, he can't restrain himself from dumping his anger on the bringers of bad news, and so the word goes round to keep a low profile.

Who are the victims, in school, of the Scheisskopf effect? Perhaps it's the teacher whose relationship with a group of difficult children is deterioriating, but who keeps quiet for fear of being thought incapable. Or the caretaker who's forgotten to order the toilet rolls and hopes half term will arrive before anyone notices.

How to avoid it? Not, clearly, by monotonously insisting that people are free to speak up. That's just what Scheisskopf does, to little avail. It's like the manager who intones, frequently and earnestly, that 'My door is always open.' For my money, the more you hear this, the less likely it is that the openness is more than cosmetic.

No, what matters is not so much whether the door is open or closed, but to what extent your colleagues can tell from your attitude and actions that their ideas and concerns are being accepted in a non-judgemental way.

'You were right to come to me about those children. We should have spotted it before. We're going to put some support in, and arrange for a bit of specialist input for you from the authority.'

'Jack, take an hour off. Go down to the cash and carry and get as many toilet rolls in your car as you can. Leave a packet in the boot to remind you not to do it again.'

Sense and nonsense in time management

Have you ever said: 'I was in danger of meeting myself coming back'?
The standard answer to people who get into this state is that they need to improve their time management. And, unsurprisingly, out there in the big wide world, time management is something of an industry. In education, though, there are particular constraints on the application of time management principles.

Is that me over there?

In the 2004 Sundance Award-winning film *Primer*, two engineers build a time machine, which they house on the edge of town, in one of those self-storage units. The moment you realise you're going to have difficulty following the story is when they arrive in the car park outside the units just in time to see themselves coming out earlier. (Or are they going in later? Please don't write and tell me.)

From then on, the complexities escalate to a level which is keeping nerdy individuals across the world happily preoccupied on the internet. Just type 'Primer film plot' into Google to see what I mean. (One critic said of the film when it was released: 'Anybody who claims they fully understand what's going on in Primer after seeing it just once is either a savant or a liar.')

The more I watched this deeply annoying (but mercifully short) movie, the more I became convinced that it ought to be used as a training video for heads and deputies about how to be in two places at once without meeting yourself coming back.

It certainly wouldn't be any less useful than some of the time management advice you come across. The bucket of rocks theory (sometimes disguised as the pickle jar theory) is a popular one. The idea is that you put big rocks in a bucket (they're your important principles), then you fill up first with pebbles, then with sand, then with water – these are smaller, increasingly unimportant tasks. The idea is that if you put the pebbles or sand or water in first, there's no room for the rocks. Anyway, it means you should give priority to what matters most. I think.

For teachers and heads, time management advice often seems difficult to reconcile with reality. That's because whatever else happens, there's always this large group of children to be looked after. People on the outside often don't seem to understand that. They wonder why we don't answer the phone, or read our emails. They urge heads to delegate jobs, forgetting that the people down the delegation line are already fully occupied with a teaching timetable.

That said, the best advice about time management I've seen comes from consultant Harold Taylor. I like his realistic approach, and the way he cuts through the myths. Here are just three of his many tips, paraphrased by me.

Don't write lists of things to do because they just tell you that you haven't done them yet. Instead, write actual slots in your diary to do them.

And one that will resonate with heads and school administrators alike.

Don't complain that interruptions – visitors, phone calls, meetings – are a waste of your time. They're part of your job. The real timewasters are self-inflicted – procrastination, searching for lost stuff, spending time on trivialities.

Finally, something I've always believed.

Don't try to change your ways with a paper or electronic personal organiser. People who use them are well-organised already. If you can get yourself sorted, a cheap notebook or diary's good enough.

See what I mean? This is someone who understands real people.

www.taylorintime.com

Status doesn't always come with competence

Heads are assumed to be perfect teachers, aren't they? They're certainly supposed to be capable of keeping order in the classroom. In fact, though, there's no obvious reason why they should be more effective either as teachers or as disciplinarians than any other capable member of staff. Which is simply to say that they are human beings, with human frailties. At times it's good to acknowledge this.

Feet of clay

Ever heard of A.J. Wentworth, BA? A fictional schoolmaster, Mr Wentworth was the central figure in a long series of gently funny – and still popular – school stories created in *Punch* articles in the thirties, by H.F. Ellis. (They're still available in book form.) The running joke is that whereas Mr Wentworth thinks he is control of his classes, it's plain to the reader that the boys are sending him up rotten. Here's just a taste – part of a huffy memo from Wentworth to the headmaster.

> Sir,
> I have not given up what might have been the best years of my life to Burgrove in order to have my boot-laces tied to the legs of my desk at the end of it and so be prevented from rising to my feet when parents are shown into the classroom …

For me, the stories sometimes make painful reading, because I was never a natural disciplinarian. I managed well enough, using learned techniques, but class control didn't come to me naturally, as it does to some.

And, I might say, I always had to solve my problems unaided. In fact I always had the feeling that any failings of mine were quietly welcomed by those who needed to see other people doing worse than themselves.

That sort of disciplinary *Schadenfreude*, once quite common, damaged morale, undermined professional integrity and, ultimately, held back children's learning.

It's not like that now – not in most places anyway. One of the most heartening changes in school life in recent years has been the way that in good schools classroom behaviour has become a whole-school issue. Where the problem's been cracked, it's been by applying a set of unified and consistent guidelines all across the institution.

One approach, for example, is to set up a specialised group of very successful teachers – measured not by hearsay and subjective opinion but by graded classroom observation and pupil performance – whose task is to take on the support of colleagues referred either by themselves or by their heads of department. Such support groups will, typically, consist of teachers from across the whole school, and they won't all by any means be in senior positions, so there's clear recognition that teaching ability, including class control, doesn't necessarily correlate with hierarchical position.

The last obstacle to making a policy like this work, though, is lack of honesty, and that's something that needs personal commitment all the way up the hierarchy. Teachers need to be reassured that they can be frank about which children, which incidents, which lessons and activities are giving them problems, and be able to discuss frankly what might be done to help.

And this, I suggest, is where senior and longer-serving colleagues should be setting the example – and don't tell me that none of you are having trouble, because I won't believe it. There are able head teachers who struggle with some of their teaching groups.

So when the behaviour policy's on the agenda – as it always is sooner or later – then, as a worldy-wise veteran, be sure not only to offer advice but also to front up and confess the areas where you could do with a bit of support. That way, the struggling NQT who feels defeated and isolated will be encouraged to speak up. A bit of honesty could well make the difference that will keep an uncertain colleague in good spirits and committed to the job.

The Papers of A.J. Wentworth, BA (1949) by H.F. Ellis is currently published by Prion Humour Classics.

Leaders under pressure may be signalling for help

Every leader needs support. Sometimes it's more than that, and they need actual help to get through a crisis. Not all leaders are capable of confessing when they're in trouble. What emerges may be a coded distress signal that an astute middle leadership needs to recognise and respond to.

It was never about the strawberries

Every deputy head, senior teacher and subject leader should read, if they haven't yet done so, Herman Wouk's *The Caine Mutiny*. Failing that they should watch the 1954 film, with Humphrey Bogart superb as Captain Queeg. Why? Because it's a marvellous and universally relevant tale of a leader who's stressed beyond his limits and ultimately falls apart.

The novel covers much more ground than the film, which confines itself to what for me is the main theme – the story of a leader who fails, and subordinates who show their own kind of weakness.

The central events happen in the Pacific in the Second World War. Queeg arrives on the ship – the battered veteran USS *Caine* – ready to tighten everything up and restore discipline.

At first his officers quite welcome this, but as time goes on, Queeg is revealed as a weak commander, lashing out at trivialities in an attempt to preserve respect. His mental state is demonstrated in several ways – he disciplines a sailor whose shirt is hanging out, and also the responsible officer. Then there's what's referred to as the 'strawberries incident', when Queeg believes that the wardroom's strawberries have been sneakily eaten by someone, and he pushes through a relentlessly obsessional and absurd quest to find the culprit, and discover how it was done. (He's sure there must have been a duplicate key to the locked fridge, and gets bogged down in a fruitless search for it.)

Officers start to be worried that a ship in combat is being badly led. At one point, when the ship is in harbour with the Pacific Fleet, senior officers, who are keeping a log of Queeg's behaviour, decide to go to the admiral with their evidence. However, they lack the courage of their convictions and when they climb the ladder to the deck of the flagship and come face to face with the full pomp and ceremony of the navy, they realise what they're up against and they change their minds.

Eventually, back at sea, in a moment of crisis, when Queeg makes a faulty decision in a heavy storm that seems likely to endanger the ship, he is relieved of his command by two officers, put up to it largely by one more junior – Lieutenant Keefer, played by Fred MacMurray – who is an amateur psychologist and is sure that Queeg is clinically paranoid.

Inevitably, back on shore, the two who relieved the captain (but not the more junior Keefer, who manages to scramble away from any blame) are court-martialled for mutiny. They seem sure to be found guilty – no military organisation can countenance the seizure of command by juniors under any but the clearest and most pressing of circumstances. However, under pressure in court from Barney Greenwald, the counsel defending the mutineers, Queeg crumbles to a pathetic wreck. The film's image of Bogart, rambling, distracted, rolling two ball bearings in his hand, is one of the great cinematic moments.

Greenwald hates himself and his two clients for this. He's sure that Keefer, who escaped charges, is the person who should have been in dock, and he has sympathy for Queeg, a man who's been at war since the fighting began.

The story has many messages, but the main one is that here is a senior leader, with a proud record, who is brought down by what we would now call stress – an inadequate word to describe the pressure on a ship's captain in the Pacific War. At the very moment that he needs help – indeed all but pleads for it to the extent that his position permits – those around him, led by Keefer, choose instead to make gossiping fun of him and, ultimately, to destroy him.

Herman Wouk's story is as clear and moral as a parable. It's about humanity and compassion, and the fact that they are qualities that can and should outweigh considerations of hierarchy and authority.

What does it tell us about leadership in school?

Well, just translate the whole thing to a school setting. Imagine a head teacher beset by problems, becoming ill-tempered, unpredictable, difficult to deal with. He's struggling to raise achievement, and to improve discipline. The local authority is breathing down his neck, and

Ofsted might arrive at any moment. Some of his decisions are hasty, almost panicky, and colleagues shake their heads and gossip.

Then, at one point during a senior leadership meeting he says, in a surprising outburst: 'You can't imagine what it's like doing this job. I sometimes wonder ...'

Then he checks himself: '... but never mind.'

It's a defining moment, because what he's doing is appealing for help. What matters is whether his colleagues will read it like that, or will they go off and whisper about the incident and take it as yet another sign of weakness?

The moral is, I suppose, that before you gather in groups to whisper about your leader, or make up unkind nicknames, or plot to complain directly to headquarters, or start making a diary of strange events – before you do any of these things, think instead about whether, and how, you can offer support and an understanding ear.

There are so many things you can do. You can just say, in that rather fraught meeting: 'Don't forget we're still here will you? Tell us what we can do. We're on your side in this.'

Or one of you can go in to the head's room, shut the door, and say: 'I've brought your coffee in; do you want to chat about things for a while?'

It's difficult to escape the thought, though, that the more likely response is that, as on the *Caine*, some less worthy instinct will lead to colleagues latching on to any sign of weakness. And that, of course, is a fault of human nature that we constantly preach to our children about.

Herman Wouk (1951) *The Caine Mutiny*, New York: Doubleday.

Listen impartially

As human beings we become programmed, as time goes on, to be more welcoming to some people than to others. That extends into working life, so that there are some people we avoid and some we walk smilingly to meet. If we carry on with that tendency as leaders, we then find ourselves judging people's ideas in advance – 'Ah, this is Chris's paper. I'm looking forward to reading it', 'Lordy, this is Mel's paper. It's sure to be a load of rubbish'.

But of course as leaders we have a clear duty not to be like that. It doesn't do to pre-judge the things that people tell us, or to be be impatient with apparently obvious or naïve suggestions. People who are put down too often are likely to switch off and make no contributions at all.

The Port-o-Shred

I'm sure you have a mobile phone and a PDA – maybe these days you even have a BlackBerry. Do you also, though, carry a 'Port-o-Shred'? This is a small shredder carried in front of you with a strap round the back of your neck. When someone comes up to you with a carefully prepared paper and says,

'I was hoping you'd have time to look at this ...'

You reply, 'Yes, yes, very interesting.' Bzzzzzzzzzzzz.

OK, it's not real of course. It's a gadget occasionally carried by the pointy-haired boss in the Scott Adams 'Dilbert' cartoons.

Like everything in Dilbert-world, though, it's only a slight exaggeration. Lots of bosses, including those in school, carry virtual Port-o-Shreds in the form of a propensity to ignore, or even be rude about, ideas brought to them by colleagues.

You can see how it might happen. There you are, experienced, seen it all before, been on the course, talked to the people at the curriculum development centre, clear about what's to be done. Then along comes Tiresome Terri with a naïve plan dreamed up in the bath the night before.

You try to dodge, or hear an imaginary phone ringing, or you turn aside to latch on to someone else. But it's to no avail, Tiresome Terri is there waiting for you, full of yet another wonderful idea. So you have to be polite – or at least you think you're being polite. In fact you're being very dismissive.

'Sorry, Terri. Maybe I'll have a look, but really it's all been sorted and there's a lot more to it than you could ever know.'

All that's missing is the sound of the Port-o-Shred. Bzzzzzzzzzz.

The problem is, of course, that Terri's now disillusioned and less likely to come up with anything in the future. So in terms of the development both of Terri and of your school, it's an own goal.

It doesn't have to be like that. Maybe what Terri needs is some responsibility – a job to do that will harness that creativity and put it to work. There's plenty of evidence to show that the way to preserve the enthusiasm of good young teachers is to give them responsiblity. One of the great pleasures of visiting schools where good things are going on is to see exactly this in action – relatively new teachers given space to develop ideas, and being led by heads and managers who then rightly enjoy the satisfaction that comes from nurturing talent. Early in a recent school year, for example, I was at Dartmouth School in Sandwell, where PE specialist Vicki Savage, just over two years into teaching, was telling me how she'd been made deputy head of Year 7 and encouraged to develop specialist PE skills that no one else had.

'Girls' football didn't exist before I came. Now it's in the curriculum', she said.

Now, a few months on, Dartmouth NQT mentor Anna Bennett tells me that Vicki has become acting head of year, and goes on to give numerous examples of teachers of two to three years' experience now holding down management jobs including heads of numeracy and literacy.

'Every NQT we've had for the last three years is now in a promoted post either here or in another school', she says.

Sandwell seems to be good at this sort of thing. Down the road, in the same authority, Wood Green High actually has an 'Innovations Unit', chaired by an assistant head.

'His job', says head Dame Enid Bibby, 'is to find as much weird and wonderful thinking as he can and see if it can be dragooned into fitting into school practice. He brings ideas to the leadership team for us to argue about whether or not they are feasible.'

So if someone wants to introduce a new curriculum subject, for example, there'll be questions about resourcing, staffing – and, importantly, what will have to be dropped to make room for it. It's a serious route, though, by which creative ideas can make progress.

The test of whether a school takes any part of its operation seriously is whether there's any funding involved. Dame Enid's Innovations Unit passes that one.

'We have a small amount of money in the budget, a bit of a magic pot, in case something needs to be supported.'

The big challenge in all of this, though, the ideal to which managers and leaders should aspire, isn't so much to make colleagues feel good and valued when their ideas are adopted – that bit's easy – but to maintain their confidence and commitment when their plans sink out of sight. At Wood Green, very clearly, people are always going to feel that their ideas are being taken seriously.

'It's to do with emotional intelligence', says Dame Enid. 'If you're prepared to find time to sit down and say it was a brilliant idea, but these are the problems – if you say, "knowing all this would you go with it if you were me?", then most people are happy.'

For her, it's giving time and attention that's important.

'What you don't want to do is discourage people. A school only changes because of new ideas, and we'd rather they came from inside than be imposed on us.'

Make sure the message is clear

Any organisation – certainly including schools – has within it eager and ambitious people who are on the look-out for ways of pleasing the leadership. They'll try to second guess the boss's plans, coming up with answers to half-formulated questions and sometimes embarking on initiatives with a view to revealing them when they're successfully running. School leaders clearly have to beware of this tendency.

What did he actually say?

In Episode 1 of the excellent BBC political comedy *The Thick of It*, the fictional Cabinet minister Hugh Abbott decides to create an agency for catching benefit cheats. He's actually in the official car, on the way to launch what he's dubbed, in tabloid-friendly style, his 'Snooper Squad' in a major speech, with the media on high alert, when he discovers that maybe the Prime Minister isn't as squarely behind the idea as he thought.

What happens is that the government's fearsome piranha-chops enforcer Malcolm Tucker (the Alastair Campbell role, wonderfully played by Peter Capaldi) detects, in conversation with Abbott, that, just possibly, the PM wasn't as definite as Abbott assumed him to be. He leaps unerringly on the flaw.

'What did he actually say, Hugh? What were the Prime Minister's actual words?'

Tucker, you see, knows perfectly well how the PM works, floating ideas here and there. He is very aware of the danger of going off at half-cock. The car stops; Tucker and Abbott and other minions spill out on to the pavement and continue the argument by the roadside.

'Well', says the hapless Minister for Home Affairs, realising even as the feeble words emerge from his lips that he's comprehensively stuffed, 'he said it was the sort of thing we should be doing.'

Who's to blame here? Hugh's been guilty of what's variously called 'exceeding his authority', or 'jumping the gun', or 'going off message' – the wide choice of terms indicates how common it is. The PM, for his part, has played the equally familiar trick of both offering and withholding support at one and the same time – deploying what you might call the 'I agree with you up to a point' leadership strategy.

Does it happen in school? You bet. How many times have you known a leader nod and say those very words – 'This is the sort of thing we should be doing'? Sometimes that's not at all what's meant. The leader is just too feeble to come out and say: 'Absolutely no chance of ever going down that route. Forget it.'

(I worked for a head once who would use the phrase 'I agree with that to some extent', which actually meant 'It's not going to happen.')

It's yet another example of a leader's reluctance to be straight with his or her colleagues – too ready to tell them what they want to hear.

I know of another head – now dead – who exemplified this 'tell them what they want to hear' philosophy to a degree that ultimately poisoned relationships in the school. Ironically, he was far from being a sinister figure of obvious Machiavellian intent. In fact, he was a genial, gregarious soul, entirely without malice. But what he did have within him was the fatal flaw of desiring above all things to be popular. To that end he would go around being friendly with everyone – and, worse, attempting to preserve his position by making sure that he told each person and group that, yes, he would do his best to see that they got what they most desired.

Then, to cement all of it, he would host convivial evenings in the pub at his own expense. And at after-school meetings for senior staff there would always be wine.

What he didn't realise was that, although yes, there was popularity of a sort to be gained, and the satisfaction of being at the centre of a joking crowd in the pub, the stark reality was that it would never bring the kind of popularity he craved. In fact, by gossiping with colleagues and telling different things to different people in a desperate attempt to keep everyone on-side, he was achieving the exact opposite of what he wanted.

So, as time went on, and teachers compared notes about what had been said in different meetings and informal gatherings, mistrust built up and any semblance of respect began to evaporate.

He was, in fact, a classically tragic figure – lonely, and when caught off-guard, likely to be frank about his self-generated problems. Yes, people still went with him to the pub, because he genuinely did have good stories to tell – he'd travelled widely and done a variety of jobs.

But everyone knew that the school was going nowhere with him at the helm. Maybe he needed help. Maybe he was the Captain Queeg figure discussed on page 51, giving out a coded message that he couldn't cope. If that was true, then his colleagues failed him, for they certainly were not in any mood to ride to his rescue.

One of the problems caused by heads like that, is that colleagues, especially ambitious younger ones, try to read what's required of them, and jump in with detailed plans. We've probably all experienced that. A drama teacher overestimates the head's professed enthusiasm for the avant-garde, and comes up with a production that makes the remaining hair curl on the head of the chair of governors. Or there's the outdoor activities specialist who's heard the head's stories of life in the frozen north, and assumed that it was OK for her to break the ice so the whole party could swim.

The Prime Minister (in the programme of course, not in real life – perish the thought) is at such an exalted level that he's insulated from any fallout consequent on his pusillanimous lack of clarity. Not only that, but – somewhat like God – he has an earthly mediator ready to convince the troops that everything is down to their own frailty. It's likely that the head, on the other hand, does not have protection of that quality and consequently fields some of the egg on his face.

Calling it a team doesn't make it one

A national team – in showjumping, soccer, tiddlywinks or whatever – usually consists of a varied bunch of people brought together from local teams across the country. They do some work together, but they still may hardly know each other. The saving grace, of course, is that their common purpose is very narrowly defined – within the next ninety minutes, get goals and prevent the other team from getting them. That's enough to force eleven highly talented individuals to become a team.

In school, though, the focus may not be quite so clear. Yes, we pay lip service to the idea of 'teams'. But do we always really understand what makes a team effective, and different from just a collection of people who happen to work in the same place?

Team building

A few years ago, some employees of mobile phone giant Ericsson were being taken to a conference in Athens when the bus they were travelling in was hijacked by masked men with shotguns. Luckily, someone saw what was going on and phoned the police (on a mobile of course. We aren't told the make). They arrived in full, heavily armed, gung-ho, trigger-happy, 'Lie flat on the ground!' mode.

Unfortunately – or fortunately, depending on your perspective – the 'hijacking' turned out to be a team building exercise. The terrorists were actors and the guns were fake. (That's the actors' guns. The police guns were extremely real.) The clever-clogs who organised it presumably wanted to see how people bore up under pressure – whether they'd work together, or fall apart, who would be stiff-upper-lip Noel Coward and who the cowardly, working-class Richard Attenborough (*In Which We Serve*, 1942).

As it turned out, though, the whole thing came close to being a tragedy, and Ericsson senior management had some fast and presumably red-faced talking to do.

The world of business seems fond of running bonding exercises – paintballing, white-water rafting, African drumming, extreme sports, tests involving barrels and planks of wood.

Very little of that sort of thing, though, seems to go on in education. Are we missing something? Or are we too sensible? It's not that we don't have teams, because we do. Schools have had senior management teams (SMTs) for some time, and they're gradually changing into Senior Leadership Teams (SLTs). Think of your own SLT for a moment. Can you imagine them in the woods with paintball guns? (I'll stop there for a moment and let you think about it.) Would all your lives be better if they did a bit of that?

I know what I think. I'm with those who believe that you can't forcibly give a team life outside of its purpose. Where the common purpose is clear, the bonding comes naturally. A soccer team, for example, has very specific aims. It doesn't really need any other kind of glue to hold it together. Whether the members drink together, or go pony-trekking in North Wales, is not really important. It's the same, I suggest, for your own senior leadership team. It exists to give life to a vision of what the school should be doing for its young people. If the vision's clear, shared and understood, and if the team members have the right mix of skills and personal qualities, then the bonding will follow.

Recently, I read *The Wisdom of Teams* by Jon R. Katzenbach and Douglas K. Smith. First published in 1993, and something of a classic now, it contains some good stories about successful teams, including that of the seven managers who, against huge opposition in their own company, found a way to transform the fortunes of the Burlington Northern Railroad in the USA. They thrived on adversity, supported each other, took risks. (They used the 'Jesuit principle' – 'It's much easier to ask for forgiveness than for permission.') As you read, it's not difficult to make the thought transfer, and to see instead of a group of railway managers, a team of committed leaders turning round a school that's in trouble. So much of what they had to do would be the same – doubters to be convinced, sceptical bureaucrats to be circumvented, resources to be blagged and creatively used.

And yet when it comes to school improvement we so often forget the team approach, and seem to be fixated on the solitary role of the super-head, driving a lonely and exhausting path through the jungle of difficulties and opposition. Maybe we should be thinking much more of the team as a whole. This is what the Burlington team was like:

The seven men developed a concern and commitment for each other as deep as their dedication to the vision they were trying to accomplish. They looked out for each other's welfare, supported each other whenever and however needed, and constantly worked with each other to get done whatever had to get done.

Is your SLT like that? I guess the truth is that not many are. Why is that? My guess is that it's because the Burlington team were often physically together, and were very clearly focussed on their goal. In a school, by contrast, each senior colleague has a pretty all-absorbing set of personal responsibilities. As a result, the concept of a 'team', as opposed to just the title, might not exist. Consider whether your own leadership team really is a team, or whether it's actually more of a weekly gathering that for some is actually a bit of a distraction, because they have individual concerns they feel they should be getting on with.

Katzenbach and Smith place great store by a team being mutually accountable, and point out the difference between 'The boss holds me accountable' and 'We hold ourselves accountable'.

'The first case can lead to the second'; they write, 'but without the second there can be no team.'

Headship is becoming almost too onerous for one person. We all acknowledge that. Perhaps it's time, therefore, to look at whether it's possible to make the leadership team into a true team rather than just a weekly meeting of people with separate responsibilities. The rewards in terms of creating a real powerhouse of combined talent and commitment at the heart of the school would be considerable. It wouldn't be easy to do, but it's just possible, isn't it, that if some of the driving energy that characterises the transforming head was put into creating a real, mutually accountable, mutually supportive and visionary senior leadership team, then wondrous things might come about.

Jon R. Katzenbach and Douglas K. Smith (1993) *The Wisdom of Teams: Creating the High-Performance Organization*, London: McGraw-Hill.

Hierarchy shouldn't breed distance

Divisions between officers and other ranks, executives and workers, white collars and blue, weekly paid and monthly, bedevil the UK workplace. It's a pity when we detect that kind of thing in our schools. I wonder, though, whether we haven't encouraged divisiveness by our emphasis on teams of leaders. The term 'senior leadership (or management) team' is potentially a divisive one in itself, and there needs to be a conscious effort to prevent it. I wonder whether leadership members themselves fully realise this, and to some extent this piece is intended to alert them.

Corridors of power

The American website 'Management-Issues.com' had a piece recently about the danger of senior managers becoming out of touch with their employees.

'Half of the 2,000 employees surveyed by HR consultancy Rightcoutts said that they have never had a conversation with their managing director while almost a quarter did not even know the name of their chief executive.'

Well, I don't think schools have reached that point yet. It's certain, though, that many teachers feel their senior management team is out of touch. A spot check on the *TES* website forums revealed 14,000 posts mentioning 'SMT', very few of them even neutral, let alone complimentary: 'twaddle we're forced to endure from smt, govt, ofsted etc'; 'demanding pupils, demanding smt, demanding parents'; 'the likes of smt continue to rant'; 'power-tripping smt'.

Is this typical of life across our schools? Maybe not, but the sheer volume of posts must be telling us something. And this at a time when 'distributed leadership' is supposedly a key principle.

So what's happening? My guess is it's all down to the growth of the notion of the leadership team, or group. Clearly, there's a lot to be said for having a team approach to leadership, but when you think about it, it seems possible that the effect, in some schools, is to increase the sense of separation between senior teachers and the rest. Put half a dozen people together and call them 'leadership' or 'senior management' and the danger is that they'll spend more time looking inwards, attending to each other, and less time looking out for and listening to the people they're supposed to be leading. Regular and frequent SMT meetings, for example, always attended by the same key people, may keep leadership figures away from the realities of school life, and encourage an atmosphere of secrecy, rumour and resentment.

What the 'leadership team' may generate, in fact, is what we might call the 'top corridor' or 'executive floor' effect. This is very common in large business organisations, and it's where there's a sharp and visible division between the decision-makers and the also-rans. The executives inhabit their own world of mystery, while the people who do the hard work have to pick up what bits of information they can. It's fertile ground for rumours – spread, often, by people who move between the two worlds – secretaries, messengers, cleaners. More importantly it's a recipe for the kind of divisiveness illustrated by those *TES* website postings.

Do we really want that in school? Of course not. So what's to be done? Well, I've noticed two things about schools where leadership figures are liked and respected. First, the number of SMT meetings has been cut to the bone, replaced by focused working parties made up of volunteers from all levels.

And, second, the leaders are out and about. The head's constantly on the corridor, marching across the field, standing in the dinner queue, visiting classrooms, setting an example for senior colleagues and unapologetically causing problems for the secretary who's trying to field calls from people wanting to speak to the head. As that same Management Issues article has it: 'Some of the most admired and successful leaders display a gritty determination not to lose touch with their staff, regardless of how large the organisation is'.

Job satisfaction really does count

What does it mean to be happy at work? Is it about making progress up the ladder? Giving customer satisfaction? Getting on with colleagues?

I suppose it's all of those, but in any case there's no doubt that if people are unhappy, then you can count on the fact that at least a large part of the problem will lie with the leadership.

Happy at your work?

My father worked in the mining industry for fifty-two years, from age thirteen to sixty-five. For nearly fifty of those years he was a driver – first a chauffeur for the coal owner, then after nationalisation in 1947, a general driver for the National Coal Board. There was no question of promotion because there was no job to which he could step up. So for all those years he didn't have a 'career' in any normal sense. He did, though, like his work and his colleagues, several of whom had become old and close family friends. The management, I realised belatedly at his funeral, had enormous respect for him. He had a lot of pride in doing his job well, and a lot of fun along the way, so maybe career and ambition and moving up aren't as important as we think.

He had many sayings, and one of them was this question that he asked people all the time.

'Are you happy at your work?' he'd say. Sometimes he was serious, sometimes ironic, and sometimes it was just a version of 'hello'. It clearly, though, expressed how he felt about the importance of being content at work.

Now, because I have become my father, as we all do, 'Are you happy at your work?' has become my signature question, and for me too it's serious or not, depending on the who, where and when. Underneath it all, though, is the same conviction that my father held, which is that to relish your job, to look forward to seeing your colleagues, and to know that whatever happens you can handle the task and be appreciated, are things are to be cherished because, sadly, they are rare in this troubled society of ours.

Job satisfaction has been proved time and again to be much more important than money, or indeed than power and status. For school leaders that should come as both a relief and an encouragement – because although they only have limited powers of renumeration, they do have lots of opportunities to make their colleagues' working lives more pleasant.

I thought of that when I read of the Gallup Organisation's twenty-five-year-long investigation into what makes what they called 'a strong workplace' – one where people are content and effective. (Take note of both words, and how they go together.)

They interviewed a million workers, asking each one hundreds of questions. Then they applied a battery of statistical analyses, discarding, refining. In the end they came up with just twelve key questions that by massive agreement measure workplace satisfaction. As you read them, imagine the people at every level for whom you are responsible asking them of themselves. How does that you make you feel? Is there any guilt there? Are you doing your best? Just consider whether you, as a leader in a school or a department, or a year group, feel that there are any areas where you could make a difference if you tried a bit harder.

> Do I know what is expected of me at work?
> Do I have the materials and equipment I need to do my work right?
> At work, do I have the opportunity to do what I do best every day?
> In the last seven days, have I received recognition or praise for good work?
> Does my supervisor seem to care about me as a person?
> Is there someone at work who encourages my development?
> Do my opinions seem to count?
> Am I made to feel that my work is important?
> Are my co-workers committed to doing quality work?
> Do I have a best friend at work?
> In the last six months have I talked with someone about my progress?
> At work, have I had opportunities to learn and grow?

(*First Break All the Rules*, by Marcus Buckingham and Curt Coffman)

After I wrote this I thought about my father again, and how he would have answered the questions. I realised that with the possible exceptions of the ones that implicitly assume a notion of progress and promotion, he would have been able to say 'yes' to every one. His supervisor did care about him. He did have a best friend at work. He did know what was expected ... and so on. So someone in that corner of the Yorkshire Coalfield, at least, was exercising the right kind of leadership.

Marcus Buckingham and Curt Coffman (1999) *First Break All the Rules: What the World's Greatest Managers Do Differently*, New York: Simon & Schuster.

Let people out of their ruts occasionally

The expression 'A change is as good as a rest' is sometimes abused, and used as an excuse. And of course, if the change means you're going to jail instead of being a member of Parliament, then you have to talk fast to bring conviction to the idea. At the same time, I'm convinced that some tired and jaded teachers, the ones who start to think of retiring early, could be retained in the profession if only they were offered something different and creative to do, even just for a short time.

As good as a rest

The other week I met a teacher of many years' service who'd just had a rejuvenating experience. Moving rapidly on, let me explain that in her case the extra spring in the step was brought about by a period of time away from her regular timetable, renewing an acquaintance with a curriculum subject, and an age group, both of which she'd left behind long ago.

Trained in music, she'd spent her early years in a music department. Career advancement, though, has taken her into a job where her major responsibility is with – and the shorthand word is mine, not hers – 'difficult' pupils in Key Stage 4 in a very challenging school.

It's a job she's good at – how could she possibly do it otherwise? And it has its own satisfactions. She's clearly the kind of person who's admired, respected and listened to by people at all levels of the organisation. At the same time, the role is demanding beyond the imagination of most of us.

Then came this opportunity. For a two-week period, the regular timetable was heavily modified while the school rehearsed a multimedia all-singing, all-dancing show to celebrate a major anniversary. Her part in the jamboree was to work with a group of Year 7s as they composed and recorded a set of their own songs for the occasion. Going back to music, and meeting younger children in an atmosphere of creative enthusiasm was as good as being on holiday. It started her thinking, too, that maybe her specialist skills could be used in her work with the older boys and girls.

She wasn't the only person – adult or child – who found something special in the experience. Senior management, clearly, now has some ideas to chew over – not least that professional development has many facets and sometimes comes heavily disguised as something else. There's a further lesson, too, in the fact that it doesn't have to be the head who has an idea like this in the first place. There are times, in the middle of stressful departmental or year-group meetings, or even in the pub after parents' evening, when a well-judged 'Tell you what. Why don't we …?' will strike fertile ground. Just remember that you may need to be generous – able to accept that the flower when it eventually blooms may be different from the one you had in mind, and could have been tended by hands other than your own.

Every member of staff matters equally

In a school with many departments and areas of work, it's easy for some people to be below the radar of the senior leadership, unnoticed and unknown. And yet there's no need for it to be like that. Many head teachers make a point of walking their whole building regularly – once a week, maybe more, maybe less, but it's the regularity that counts. Sometimes, though, I suspect that they're taking more notice of the building – a crack in the wall here, some chewing gum on the carpet there – than they are of the people working in it. To that extent, I wonder if a virtual tour of the building plan might not be just as useful. You sit with the plan, you put your finger on every room or space and you say to yourself: 'Who works there? What's their name? Who is their line manager? When did I last have a discussion about them?'

Sometimes that would be easy. Other times – imagine a science prep room, or a section of the kitchen – you'd be forced to think a bit, which as this piece shows, would be no bad thing.

Passing by on the other side

I met a dinner lady during the recent holiday. She described herself that way, but actually she's a cook, making and serving dinners in a big comprehensive. She talked a lot about her work, and it soon became clear that what she really wanted to do was to offload her feelings about being bullied at work. Her supervisor, she said, picks on every aspect of her work, tries to turn the other women against her (they're sympathetic but powerless) and generally makes her life a misery.

'I dread going to work', she said.

The phrase rang a bell with me. Long ago, when I was a child in South Yorkshire, I remember my father's youngest brother – also bullied at work, as I later discovered – saying to my dad:

'I fair dread of a morning.'

His exact words and his anxious face are clear in my mind, and in later years I've continued to use the memory as a measure of what's tolerable and what isn't in a person's working life. So when anyone – a friend, a colleague, my daughter – is down and disheartened about work, I always say, 'On Sunday night, do you dread the thought of Monday morning?'

And I mean dread here. I don't count the mild Sunday night blues that we've all had. I mean the sick feeling that makes your supper tasteless and overshadows everything and in the end is going to keep you awake and feeling doubly bad next day.

'If it's like that,' I say, 'it's time to do something about it. Life is too short and too precious to let it go on.'

As leaders, are we sure we'd know if any of our colleagues was feeling like that? Are we equipped to find out, and to do anything about it?

The dinner lady who sparked off these thoughts is nearly sixty. Why should she have to take the sort of crap she is enduring day by day? Is there no one in her school who can see what's happening and offer her some advice and moral support?

I suppose the answer is that nobody notices. Senior staff hardly ever set foot in the kitchen, other teachers just peer through the serving hatch and exchange pleasantries with the people working there as they collect their lunches. And, after all, the service is run from outside the school directly by a department of the local authority. That, though, doesn't mean it isn't part of the school family – or rather it shouldn't mean that. Certainly this lady felt that the school should be in a position to protect her.

I don't think this is entirely a matter of procedures and lines of management in any case. I believe that an experienced teacher, presumably, with some clout around the place, ought to be able to spot when a person's in trouble, and be ready to lend an ear and give support. You don't have to be a counsellor, or an advocate. The person who needs help is often demoralised into inaction and just needs someone to say: 'Take control. Make things happen!' It might be something really simple – 'Contact the union. You pay enough in subs after all.' Or 'Talk to the deputy, I know her, and she'll listen to you.'

We're ready to tell our children, after all, to speak up about their problems.

Build on strengths

It's easy to write off people who seem out of date, tired and resistant to change. Real leadership, though, involves working to everyone's strengths, so that nobody's left out in the cold, disgruntled and resentful. This is a very real issue in today's schools. Early retirements are less readily available than they once were, and it's very common for a new head, brought in to stir things up, to find that there's a minority of people who are stuck in their ways, reluctant to change. What's the leader to do? Wring hands and complain? Try to sack people? Complain to the authority? None of those are very positive, and hardly to be expected of someone who's presumably been chosen because of their above-average leadership skills.

Jurassic psychology

A head confided to me that he had taken over a school which had 'dinosaurs' (his word) on the staff. It was the archetypal 'coasting' school when he arrived – nice area, polite children, and one or two teachers who had been there forever with no intention of either leaving or changing.

'It's always negative', said this head. 'Nobody wants to move things on.'

(This is probably unfair to dinosaurs. They were around for 160 million years, and did plenty of evolving during that time. Still, we know what we mean.)

I was reminded, when I heard this, of Mr Jones (let's call him that), sadly dead now, who had taught in the same classroom of a midlands secondary school for almost the whole of his career. His teaching methods remained largely unchanged for the whole of that time.

A great believer in discipline, Mr Jones saw himself as a bulwark against a rising tide of anarchy. He liked to take assembly, because it gave him the opportunity to bring the whole school to heel a bit. The traditional definition of assembly – 'A hymn, a prayer and a bollocking' – might well have been coined with him in mind.

His way of encouraging hymn singing, for example, was to stand, frozen faced, arms folded, silently listening to what amounted to tentative groaning set to music. Then, after a verse or so he would shout 'Stop!' and deliver one of a selection of diatribes, the best one being,

'You can make plenty of noise for the Rolling Stones. Now let me hear what you can do in the presence of Almighty God!'

So what's to be done about dinosaurs?

The first thing, I guess, is to question the label. We're pretty quick with labels and stereotypes aren't we? Once Mr Jones, or the teachers in their coasting school are labelled as 'dinosaurs' – or simply as 'negative people' or 'obstructive', or 'don't want to know' – then the danger is that everything they say and do will be seen in that light. From that point the whole thing becomes self-fulfilling – exactly as it does with children.

For wise words about this, look at the 'Ask Siggy the Shrink' website, where someone pleads:

'Help me with people who are ALWAYS negative.'

The answer includes this advice:

> Remember that when you use big generalizations like always, never, everybody, nobody, etc. in what you say, they usually reflect big generalizations in your thoughts. Big generalizations are rarely accurate, and they can hide the details that would reveal the truth.

So part of the answer is to look beyond the catch-all judgement, and seek out the rather more complicated person behind it. That was what Mr Jones's last head teacher before his retirement did when she arrived. She listened to the warnings about him. But she kept on listening, and gradually learned a few other things about this dinosaur. That the parents respected him, for example. And, rather to her surprise, that the children quite liked the disciplined peace of his classroom, where, behind closed doors, he exhibited a degree of gruff kindness rarely seen in the staffroom (which he hardly ever entered) or the assembly hall. She discovered that he was in demand by local churches as an excellent lay preacher. She noticed, too, that after school was over, he was often still in his room with a group, running, in effect, an unofficial homework club for children who found it difficult to work properly at home. (He didn't talk much in these sessions, preferring to get on with his own work. The striking thing, though, was that the children clearly felt secure there.)

Mr Jones, she realised, though entirely comfortable in his classroom, felt resentful and threatened by changes outside it. What she had to do, instead of confronting his aggression, and adopting the 'shape up or ship out' strategy urged upon her by others, was build up his confidence and convince him that he had a significant place in her vision for the school. It was, of course, easier to have the thought than to carry it through – but that sort of challenge is what leadership is all about.

So, over a couple of years, she made a friend of Mr Jones, cashing in on his disciplinary skills, but encouraging and coaching the kindness that was always there. She sat in his church and heard him preach, and pointed out the way that his skills could be used in school. She made his homework club official – as, inspirationally, 'Study time with Mr Jones'.

So, for the final years of a long career, Mr Jones was rediscovered, both by others and by himself.

http://www.dealingwithpeople.com/dpcs/siggy/Ask.Siggy.html

Focus on the key skills when you build your team

I was useless at ball games. Something to do with being very short-sighted, I suppose – I reckon the refractive index of my spectacles was sufficient to displace the ball several centimetres away from where it really was. Well, that's my excuse anyway. The consequence was that I was always a marginal figure when it came to informal soccer games, trotting along in the wake of the action, willing the ball to go anywhere but near to me. I was thinking of that when I wrote this piece about the qualities we have in mind when we recruit teachers. Just as the only qualification for being in a football team is the ability to play well, I guess the only real qualification for being a teacher is the ability to teach. That's obvious – but we don't always behave as if it is.

I like you, but you're useless

One of my primary school memories is of lining up in the games lesson to be picked for one football team or the other. Two stars stood at the front, twin apples of the teacher's eye. They shared the available talent between them starting with the best and working their way down to me and a few other misshapen, bespectacled, scrawny (or the opposite), buck-toothed also-rans. We weren't really picked at all. There came a point where the two teams just trotted off, leaving us to tag on at the end as we wished. We could all have joined the same team had we wanted, for neither captain felt that our presence registered in any way. And the fact that my mother had rigged me out in glaringly brand new top-grade football boots only made things worse.

Much later in life, though, I realised that what was going on constituted an object lesson in how to put together an effective team of people. Only one criterion was in operation – that of being good at the basic ball skills of soccer. There was no interview, no aptitude test. The judgement was based entirely on first-hand observation over time. Neither was there any question of 'Will this person fit in with the others?' or 'Can lack of ability be balanced by enthusiasm and eagerness to learn?' Not even friendship counted. I know, because I was a firm friend of one of the regular choosers, and in that pitiless ritual our relationship meant nothing at all.

Of course, once the team was in action, rifts and arguments and prima-donna tantrums broke out. Always, though, the clarity and urgency of the prime objective soon damped them down.

Maybe the lesson really is that straightforward – that if you want school improvement you forget all the stuff about compatibility and potential, level of paper qualification, place in the hierarchy, and just choose people who are known to have a robust and verifiable history of excellence in the classroom. Any emerging problems – clumsiness in personal relationships, lack of experience in running a department, halitosis – should lie well within the capabilities of a good senior leadership team.

A bit extreme I suppose – but it's still true that it's too easy, when we're recruiting staff, or putting together working teams in school, to be distracted from the importance of the core business of teaching and learning.

Listening and really listening

We pay lip service to the notion of 'being a good listener'. In truth, though, it's a difficult skill. There's much more to it than just hearing. Real listening means being drawn into the other person's thoughts, processing them and taking them on board – and then reaching out for more. Poor listening is often a defence mechanism – a feeling that you can't bear someone else to be treading on your territory.

I say, I say, I say

Have you ever tried to tell a joke to a D-list comedian? I have, and, I have to tell you, it turned out to be exactly the wrong thing to do.

The one I tried my joke on is a club comic – by which I mean Wheeltappers and Shunters rather than Jongleurs. He's the kind who has to be the centre of attraction. You've met him – relentlessly hilarious off stage as well as on, often at the expense of his long-suffering wife. I was in this particular joker's company one night and, emboldened by drink (how many disasters have started with that phrase), I began to tell him one of the excellent Yorkshire miners' jokes I've inherited from my dad. I thought I'd be doing him a service – adding to his repertoire maybe.

Well, let me tell you, 'lead balloon' hardly covers it. Basically, he just stared at me and carried on as if nothing had happened. At that point I realised that for him, simply by the act of owning a joke, let alone telling one (I made no pretence at performance), I represented competition. I guess that had I finished the joke, he might well have stolen it for himself. Comedians are good at that. (Which A-list comic was known as 'the Thief of Bad Gags'? Answer below.)

Better comedians, of course, take material from wherever it arrives, bending it, shaping it, rooting around its assumptions, often rejecting it –

but always, at the very least, listening to it. The non-listening comedian, by contrast, is probably doomed to self-destruction.

Transfer to the world of work that same self-obsessive fear of taking on other people's ideas, though, and the devastation may well be spread more widely.

One of the most common organisational non-listening symptoms starts with the fervent conviction, in any gathering, that you must always know more about the subject under discussion than the person currently speaking. We all suffer from it to some extent. Confess now, were you ever in a gathering where you felt impatient for the current speaker to finish? Did you lean forward, fidgeting, uttering urgent little grunts and generally waiting impatiently for an opportunity to get into the act? Of course you did. But the saving grace is that you felt bad about it later, and tried not to do it next time.

If it's like that among friends and colleagues, consider what it's like when the leader suffers from the same syndrome. What you get then is something like this account, from the 'Listening Leadership' website (www.listeningleader.com) of how a non-listening boss handles a meeting: 'If I, or anyone else, says something, he simply says our name over and over until we shut up and let him talk.'

You can easily put yourself there can't you? Trying to make a point while the person at the head of the table is bouncing with impatience, chanting: 'Sam ... yes ... Sam ... but Sam ... now Sam, Sam, Sam ... listen Sam ... '

You've been in that meeting I guess. Probably yesterday or the day before. It's demeaning, debilitating and in the end is going to stifle the flow of ideas.

The leader's listening has to be genuine, of course. It can't be an impatient going-through-the-motions charade – the sort of 'consultation' that, in so many areas of life, has given the word itself a bad name.

Various writers have identified 'levels of listening', from hearing up to paying careful attention perhaps. I've tried to distil my own four levels, appropriate, I think, to the task of leadership.

- Level one. You aren't listening at all. In fact the only reason you don't interrupt is because you're restrained by the residual power of the good manners your mum taught you.
- Level two. You force yourself to hear the words and the ideas, but all the time you're working out why they don't fit your preconceptions.

- Level three. You realise that the person speaking knows more about the subject than you do, and you're trying to think how to respond in a way that will preserve your dignity.
- Level four. With rising interest, you become eager to know more about what the person is saying.

The daddy of all management gurus, Peter Drucker, was effectively describing level four when he wrote, forty years ago, of 'consistently listening with genuine curiosity'.

It's 'curiosity' that's important here – not just being aware that the other person knows something useful, but having a real drive to discover what it is and to pick away at the detail. Drucker developed this further, pointing out that the effective leader actively seeks views contrary to his or her own, and then delves down into the reasons for them.

(Stop here for a moment. Consider whether the leaders you know, including yourself, actually go out to solicit opposing views, trying to understand what lies behind them. How many political leaders do this? Come to that, how does the concept of 'conviction' as a leadership principle chime with it? In this regard it's interesting that Al Gore, narrowly defeated by George W. Bush for the US Presidency in 2000, while declining in later years to call President Bush 'stupid', used the term 'incurious'.)

The contributor of the Listening Leadership story, quoted earlier, went on with his complaint, and made what is surely the clinching argument for being a listening leader: 'The most knowledgeable people in our company are the employees. When our leader won't let any of us finish a sentence, I wonder who he believes he is leading.'

Apply this statement to schools and it rings true as a bell. The head who doesn't listen to teachers, who believes that his or her hard-won expertise must automatically be worth more than the daily refreshed experience of people directly engaged in the classroom, is surely on the road to self-delusion.

Peter F. Drucker (1996) *The Effective Executive*, London: Harper Collins.
Thief of Bad Gags. Bob Monkhouse, allegedly.

Valuing your people

We're all guilty of taking people for granted – not fully appreciating what they have to offer, perhaps even doing the opposite and homing in on their limitations. Just because somebody can't get to meetings in the evening, or isn't very keen on computers, doesn't necessarily mean that they're in the way of progress, does it? A talented and dedicated teacher is worth keeping, even if it means making some compromises. And in any case, loyalty works both ways – or should do.

Goodbye old friend

I went to a retirement do not long ago. It was the usual bittersweet event, both a celebration and an acknowledgement of the loss of yet another experienced teacher.

Joan (not her real name) had been a teacher for thirty years, twenty-five of them in the same school, mostly running the Reception class.

In her early years she was a human dynamo, up for anything. She ran a gym club, she was teacher rep on the PTA – a job which her predecessor gave up with relief. Everything was set fair and she seemed destined to become a deputy, well on the road to headship. She'd have been good at it too. Then everything changed, because her mother sadly and quite suddenly became heavily dependent on her.

Joan had to see her mother, who lived alone a couple of miles from school, three and sometimes four times every day. She called in on her way to school, she popped round at lunchtime, she saw her on the way home, and almost every evening she returned to her at bed-time.

It ran poor Joan ragged and inevitably her career came to a halt. It was difficult to get to after-school or lunchtime meetings and although she tried to get to the courses and briefings on new developments and initiatives, she only managed by dint of a whole lot of juggling involving understanding neighbours and a certain amount of tearfulness on her mother's part. She never made it to the staff Christmas party – 'I want to be at the children's play,' she'd say, 'and I can't do both.'

Inevitably, Joan was drowning in an ocean of guilt – about her mother, about not keeping up with developments, about letting down her colleagues. Nobody saw her smile any more.

What she never did feel guilty about, though, was her performance at the core activity for which she was employed. She was – and she knew it – a gifted teacher of young children. They loved her and she made them want to learn. The parents were relieved when their children were put into her care, and weren't averse to trying to wheedle them in when they weren't. Nobody could remember her having a day off, and she often said that it was teaching that kept her sane – and she meant that more literally than many assumed.

That's why she resisted giving the job up for so long. For a long time she'd worked with a head who knew how difficult things were for her. He did his best to help, not worrying if she didn't make it to morning briefings, making sure she had time to go home at lunchtime, not leaning on her for courses and meetings.

'Joan,' he said to her once, when she was apologising, yet again, for not getting to a meeting, 'you're the rock that keeps us steady. All the way up to Year 6 we can tell which kids were with you in Reception.'

Inevitably, though, things changed. The old head retired. A new one came with a strong improvement brief from the governors. At the same time, new teachers came, with the time and enthusiasm to give that she'd once had. Joan could tell that they weren't all that sympathetic when she had to leave early from meetings, or couldn't get to evening planning sessions, with wine and sandwiches, at a coordinator's home.

Then came the hints that if she wanted to retire there might be a deal on (or under) the table. Joan sighed, because she knew that people only had the interests of the school at heart. She was really reluctant to be parted from her children and her teaching, though.

Still, in the end, it all became too much. One more new initiative, an Ofsted inspection that caused questioning and upheaval in the school, and she couldn't face going on.

They praised her fulsomely at her retirement do. The Chief Education Officer said warm things. They gave her garden furniture, and told her to have a good holiday. Maybe a cruise? Keep in touch now!

Afterwards, she told her mother about it. 'And the good thing is, mother, I'll be able to see much more of you now.'

Good teachers have lives beyond the job

Adverts for teaching jobs used, quite often, to specify an 'experienced teacher'. That's not so common now, as requirements become much more specific. The phrase is still alive and well, though, in professional conversation, carrying with it a note of approval as if 'experienced' is synonymous with 'good', which it plainly is not. There's experience and then there's experience, and that's something I've tried to unpick here.

How's your hinterland?

High up on every head's list of nightmare moments is the one where a veteran teacher responds to an Ofsted inspector's question by tapping his forehead and saying: 'Planning? After thirty years it's all up here, my son.'

When something like this happens – and believe me it does – it acts as the complete antidote to the assumption that there's no substitute for experience. As one inspector said, reporting a similar incident to me:

'She claimed to have twenty years' experience, but really it was one year repeated twenty times.'

Even so, there are some qualities that really do take a bit of time to mature. Management gurus call it the pregnancy principle, which says that it takes nine months to make a baby and that you can't hurry the process by engaging nine women for one month.

All that was on my mind when a primary head told me recently that he was looking for a literacy coordinator. I asked him what sort of person he had in mind. I suppose I thought he'd talk about the national literacy strategy, and the literacy hour, and all the related management and leadership skills.

Knowing the man, I realise I should have known better.

'I want somebody who's been around a good length of time, reads a lot and goes to the theatre', he said.

Obvious isn't it? And yet, to my shame I was slightly taken aback.

Then I met the person, near to retirement, and a little tired, who's doing the job already, and I realised that here is someone whose lifelong love of books and literature, and understanding of the theatre, shine through everything that she does both in the classroom and in her dealings with colleagues. This is a teacher with a real feel for words and rhythm, sensitive to what children are trying to say and write, always encouraging, unerringly focused on what works well, ready to be delighted by a turn of phrase, able to suggest what the next step might be and where models of good writing are to be found.

The head, obviously, wants to replace her with someone who has the same priorities. It could be a young, relatively inexperienced person of course – it's unfair to assume otherwise. Think, after all, of those young poets and writers we bring into school to meet our children. I reckon, though, that here's a welcome opportunity for someone who's managed, over a period of time, to preserve and develop a rich cultural life outside the demands of policies, initiatives and strategies – to keep alive what Edna Healey memorably called (describing her husband Denis's many interests) 'a hinterland'.

The target police will want to know what all this has to do with children's learning. To which I'll suggest that it has absolutely everything to do with it. Literacy isn't a mechanical concept, founded in drills and skills. The mechanics are important all right – but in a teacher we ought to be able to take them for granted. What a literacy leader needs is a visible, heart-on-the-sleeve emotional commitment to the English language, demonstrated by a continuing need to be exposed to it in print, on film and on the stage.

When I wrote this in the *TES*, I called the teacher who was leaving 'she'. Really, though, it was a wise and gifted man called Paul Aston, and I wanted to make sure of his anonymity because the reason he was leaving his job was that he was terminally ill, and in fact he died shortly afterwards. Paul was the kind of teacher every head would love to have. Yes, he had that hinterland – he loved photography, the theatre, books, and as a young man he'd been a champion swimmer. What I should have pointed out in the original piece, though – and am now able to do – was that he clearly demonstrated how having the hinterland makes you into a better colleague and a better teacher. It seems to me that if you're tapped into the infinite depth and beauty of the arts, then you're wiser, more tolerant, more understanding of what makes people tick. And, I reckon, if Paul's anything to go by, you're more aware of what it means to be a teacher – a mentor with the awesome responsibility of improving the life chances of young people. At his funeral, Paul's head said that Paul was 'proudly a teacher'. What an epitaph, and what a compliment. There can be no better one.

Making best use of people

I'm fascinated by the image created in the metaphor I describe in this piece. I see a flowing stream – a babbling brook indeed – and a lot of jolly people-shaped corks rushing merrily along with the current. It's such a powerful idea, and a very sound one, based, as it is, on the notion of releasing hidden or repressed talent, to the benefit of children and their learning.

Gently down the stream

Are you a bobbing cork? When Bob Salisbury – later Sir Bob – was head of Garibaldi School in Nottinghamshire he used that expression to me as he described his approach to the development of his staff. It was so striking an image that it's stayed with me, and I've shamelessly used it many times.

What Bob was saying, you see (forgive me Bob if I've in any way misunderstood – all errors are mine) was that teachers and other colleagues shouldn't feel restricted to paths, or lines, or ladders – nothing so rigid. Rather they should see themselves moving along in a stream. Yes, they're making progress, heading onwards, but within the stream they are happily and independently bobbing – free to cross over, speed up, slow down, wander to the side for a bit, bounce off each other and ultimately, perhaps, end up in an entirely different bit of the flow from where they started.

So it was that Bob would interview staff and say to them:

'Right, you're a geography teacher. Now tell me, given total freedom, what job you really wish you could be doing in this school.'

That way, he made some remarkable discoveries, unearthed some old regrets and released a good deal of hidden talent. One young teacher, I recall, achieved a secret ambition to become head of the sixth form, and I believe at least one other opted to do more teaching and less administration.

Of course, it all took time, and called for a deal of imagination and diplomacy – but that's what Bob Salisbury was good at. He didn't become Professor Sir Bob for nothing.

The long-term effect, of course – and here's the lesson for everyone working in any school, anywhere – was to cause people to think that maybe the path they thought they were on isn't bounded by brick walls after all. Perhaps it really is possible to do something completely different.

The obvious objection – that somebody else is doing the job you fancy – is not, by the way, as final as you might think. Once everyone has started to think flexibly, a number of factors kick in. One person perhaps intends to retire next year. Another thinks a change of subject will be professionally useful. Yet another is relieved at the prospect of less responsibility. And maybe that big department could usefully be reorganised into two. It's surprising how well it can work. Can you make it happen? Nothing ventured, nothing gained.

Handling a star in the team

Inevitably, some teachers are better than others. Some, indeed, are real naturals, loved by children and parents, with an enviable ability to bring the best out of everyone. Being the leader of a team with one or more stars in it is a challenge, especially if you aim to be even-handed, thoughtful of everyone's needs.

Ready for my close-up now

Think of star soccer players – real stars, that is, people like Best, Beckenbauer, Pelé, Gascoigne. Just how important are they to their team's collective success?

The fans, of course, are in no doubt, and neither are the media. Before the 2006 World Cup, England superstar Wayne Rooney was battling to recover from injury while the nation waited with bated breath. So when a photograph appeared of Wayne doing a scissor kick on the training field, a wave of euphoria swept the nation. 'There is a God!' screamed the *Sun*.

How, though, do you think, the other players react to all of that? And how does the manager deal with it? What's it like for the 'ordinary' members of a squad (in reality, of course, exceptionally talented individuals every one) to have to deal day by day with the presence among them of someone who's widely regarded as a cut above the rest and, into the bargain, indispensable to success?

These aren't just football-related questions, because what we're discussing here is how to manage any team of individuals who are all talented, but some of whom are actually exceptional.

I had a glimpse, once, of how not to do it. I visited a primary school and the head, let's call her Mrs Ernison, took me on the standard tour. Several times she spoke warmly of one particular teacher. 'Miss Foot, absolute gem. Just wait till you see her', she said.

When we did go into the star's classroom, what attracted my attention wasn't so much the charismatic teacher, the alert children or the beautifully organised room, but the behaviour of the head. She went straight up to her protégé, looking meaningfully at me as if to say, 'Are you getting this?' and sort of melted into a display of smiles, arm-touching and head-tilting – behaviour quite different from anything I'd seen in encounters with other colleagues. It came as no surprise to discover, at lunchtime, a more or less silent staffroom, peopled by glum-looking sandwich munchers. The star wasn't there because, the head said approvingly later, she preferred to work in her classroom through lunch.

Heads aren't naïve, and it's unlikely that Mrs Ernison thinks she is doing anything more than ensuring that a key player, essential to the success of the squad – sorry, school – feels looked after and valued. Schools are remarkably vulnerable to staff changes. Two good people leaving, replaced by two not-so-good ones or by a succession of agency supply staff, can be enough to knock a high-flying school or department off course.

What Mrs Ernison is in danger of forgetting, though, is that by putting so much energy into one apparently indispensable person she runs some risks, quite apart from the obvious and very likely damage to personal and professional relationships. It seems possible, for example, that she's failing to pick up on and nurture the skills and ideas of other colleagues, some of whom undoubtedly have serious ambitions and the potential to realise them. If this is so, then not only may they lose interest and momentum, but some of them might actually leave. Either way, no matter how good Miss Foot may be, the result is likely to be a net loss of teaching quality.

The answer is to run a development programme that clearly provides equality of access to all. That's the approach of Paul Carey, managing director of consultants RSM Potential International – and soccer fan – to whom I chatted about this.

'People need to know that the same rules apply to everyone, and that each person is encouraged in the area of their strengths', says Carey.

He's very keen on working to strengths and not wasting time correcting weaknesses.

'I used to know Puskas – he coached my son when he was in Australia', he says. (Ferenc Puskas was captain of the Hungarian team that beat England 6–3 at Wembley in 1953, and 7–1 in the return match in Budapest. In a long career he became one of the greatest soccer players of all time.)

'Puskas', Carey went on, 'couldn't shoot with his right foot. But what would have been the point of spending time making him do it? He was Puskas after all.'

It seems possible that Mrs Ernison spends a lot of time thinking of weaknesses, regretting that more of her staff aren't like Miss Foot. It's an easy trap to fall into, and overcoming the mindset can be difficult. Sven-Göran Eriksson attempted to find the balance when he was manager of England's football team. He said to the *Daily Mail* once: 'Wayne Rooney is one of the best footballers in the world, but at a certain point we have 22 other players in the squad, plus stand-by players, and they are really, really good football players, absolutely.'

Or maybe you think that's one 'really' and an 'absolutely' too many.

www.rsmi.co.uk

The new broom might not be the right tool

To make a broom last longer, turn it 180 degrees frequently as you sweep. This will help keep the broom even.
('Your First Horse Care Tips – Stable Management', www.firsthorse.com)

Would you like to be a new broom? It's an attractive idea. The new school as tabula rasa, waiting there for you to write and draw upon it as you will. But then, you only have to say it to realise that it's never going to be as simple as that.

Sweeping clean

The metaphor of the new broom, sweeping into dark corners, getting rid of muck and debris, and leaving everything clean and sweet, is an alluring one. For a new head it seems particularly attractive. You walk into a school that's crying out for your deft and confident touch. Never again will you have such licence to shake things up, and in your hand – metaphorically at least – is that legendary new broom that sweeps clean.

We've all seen it. One head I knew, worried by an absence of written schemes of work, spent the summer holiday writing them himself. Come September, teachers found them all, neatly bound, on their desks when they reported for work.

Another, scandalised that teachers obviously didn't like their open-plan classrooms, went round on her first Monday evening and moved all of the bookcases and display screens they'd erected as barriers.

Good positive stuff do you think? A new dawn? Or a surefire recipe for muttering, dissent and passive resistance?

('Who does she think she is, her in her Jacques Vert?')

Well, you can already guess what I think, and I'm not alone. The feeling among thinking leaders is that the idea of the new broom is a seductive illusion. Consultant Mitch McCrimmon, in an article on the 'Suite 101' management website, calls it 'an unnecessary and costly emotional reaction'. And a paper on change in education from the University of Sydney says:

> The new broom approach with talk about 'new starts' can be rather distressing to those who may perceive the change as an end to their careers. While it can be an effective strategy when losing existing staff is a necessary element of the change needed, the consequences can be very unsettling to the staff as a whole. Sometimes the most valuable staff are those who feel most threatened by the new broom approach while the ones that were targeted for departure develop strategies to remain.

The reality is that no matter how strong the urge to put things right, there never are or were any short-cuts. You have to hold back and listen and learn. It may be that people you think of as resistant to change actually have reasons for what they're doing. And in any case, there's always a complicated set of dynamics involved – the way teachers relate to each other, the perceived characteristics of certain groups of children, even the nature of particular rooms in the building. If you're new to the school you know nothing of any of this, and you ride roughshod over it at your peril.

So wield your pristine broom with care. Don't waste it on shadows and windblown dust that'll go away on their own. Wait till you're quite certain where the real muck is.

www.edsw.usyd.edu.au/schools_teachers/prof_dev/resources/GordonStanley.pdf
businessmanagement.suite101.com/article.cfm/the_new_broom

Make sure your people have home lives

How early do you get to school? What time do you leave? More importantly, what feelings do these questions evoke? The whole business of how much time you devote to school is fraught with possibilities for resentment, guilt and envy. School leaders have a particular responsibility to navigate themselves and their colleagues through these minefields.

Please go home

Do you stay late at work? More importantly, if you're in a responsible position, do you put pressure on colleagues to stay late? Think about that, because it's possible that you don't even fully realise the demands you're making. Here, for example, is a forty-three-year-old teacher with three children in two different schools. She has to leave school no later than 4.30 p.m. – but she's never missed a pre-arranged meeting or course, and she's confident of the quality of her work. Lately, though, she's felt pushed out of the loop.

'The head is in soon after seven in the morning', she says. 'He's walking round looking at classrooms and reading children's work on the wall. He's still around twelve hours later, still walking the building. And if you pass the school on Sundays, you can see his car there.'

That's fine as far as it goes. What worries this teacher, though, is that it doesn't end there.

'He clearly wants people to talk to. I think he's lonely, which is really the problem. So if you're there in your room when he comes around, he's pleased to see you and eager to discuss everything – children's work and individual progress. And he also seems to be looking for support and approval for his plans and visions.'

As a result, those staff able to do it – and they're mostly the younger ones with no family ties – try to make sure they're there to be seen when the head does his rounds. There are Brownie points for being around early or late, or both.

'So,' our teacher goes on, 'the feeling now is that he has a clique around him – eager supporters and disciples. Sometimes they all go to the pub. Frankly, I neither have the time nor the inclination to do that – and so I feel that I, and some of the others like me, are being pushed to the margins.'

How can you avoid being that kind of leader? I found one answer in an article by management writer Penelope Trunk, in the online magazine *The Hook*. It was actually written not for managers but for their staff, and it consisted of a number of positive strategies which they can deploy to avoid having to stay late. What I've done here is adapt them – turn them around so that they become guidelines for the person in charge. Here they are – pointers for managers who want to help staff with their work–life balance.

- Concentrate on the quality of the paperwork you ask for, not the quantity. Give praise when it's concise and to the point, and make known your approval of brevity.
- Make sure your staff know exactly what's required of them, so they don't spend ages wondering, or doing extra things, 'just in case'.
- Accept 'no' when it comes from someone who already has too much to do. Assume that the person has made a considered professional decision.
- Don't make demands that will involve colleagues in weekend work – and as far as you can, try not to schedule meetings, lesson observations, handing in of planning, for Mondays.
- Make a conscious effort not to feel critical of people who don't stay late, or approving of the midnight-oil burners. It's the quality of their contribution to the school's mission that counts.
- If necessary, go around and tell people to go home, and then leave yourself.

I discussed this with Sir Kevin Satchwell, head of the highly successful Thomas Telford school in Shropshire. He tries to build a community in which people work very hard while they're in school, but aren't expected to give hours of their time afterwards.

'It wouldn't comfort me to know that I had teachers working until seven, eight, nine at night at school', he says. 'I want them to be out doing something different.'

At Thomas Telford, staff finish teaching at 4 p.m., and then stay to 5 p.m. 'You need a businesslike approach', he says. 'You work till five, using the time wisely. If you need to stay till quarter past to finish some marking, then don't take anything home.'

So there are no parents' evenings at Thomas Telford. 'What's the point,' asks Sir Kevin, 'when I give them a report every three-and-a-half weeks and they can come and see a teacher by appointment? Where else in industry would someone be expected to work all day and then stay till ten at night?'

For him, it's a matter of the head's duty of care to staff.

'The head is the gatekeeper to the staff's working conditions', he says. 'I would say that the head has a major responsibility to ensure that members of staff have a proper life outside school.'

The aim, always, is to maintain a healthy, enthusiastic team, tired at the end of the day but not exhausted and stressed. To encourage overwork, whether explicitly or by tacit acceptance, may risk the well-being of people who are vital to the school.

'What does the head do when they burn out? Where does the responsibility lie then?' he asks.

www.readthehook.com/stories/2007/06/07/brazen.aspx

Do senior leadership figures need to teach in class?

To what extent does leadership involve actually pitching in and doing the job? Should head teachers be teachers, for example? Or is that a waste of valuable management time? More to the point, perhaps, when they do teach, are they doing it for the good of the institution, or to give the children a taste of real quality, or are they just escaping from the telephone?

Pitching in

Most head teachers choose to teach some classes, even when the staffing position is such that they don't actually need to. Why is this? Are they saying 'This is how it's done'? Are they nervous about their credibility? Is it something they half-guiltily enjoy as an escape from the paperwork?

I was reminded of these questions when I learned something recently about the way army officers were supposed to behave in the First World War.

In that war, soldiers spent a lot of time digging trenches – desperate work, especially in cold driving rain with deep mud underfoot. And while it was going on, officers were supposed to stand around looking important.

Unsurprisingly, many younger officers were uncomfortable with this, and started to get stuck in. Commanders, though, were disconcerted when they found out, and some ordered their officers to stop, on the grounds that labouring would diminish them in the eyes of their men.

What these young officers had realised, though, was that when it came to the actual digging, their contribution as leaders had temporarily come to an end. To continue trying to 'lead' the diggers would surely be absurd, particularly as peacetime life for so many conscript soldiers then had involved digging.

'Come along, Smithers! Insert your spade into the ground at the regimental angle of forty-two degrees.'

'Johnson! Throw the surplus soil over your left shoulder!'

It just wouldn't do, would it? So there were only two options. They could either stand in manly poses looking on, slapping their riding crops against their boots, or they could jump down and join in. ('Cor, Sir. Wish your dad could you see you now, eh?')

Dr Todd Stephens, one of the people who led a team of volunteers cleaning up homes in New Orleans after last year's floods, puts this very well in an article in the online *DM Review*.

The actual cleaning task, he explains, which involves stripping a house down to the bare boards and walls, is hard but not complicated. The kind of people who are doing the job know perfectly well how to do it. Leadership, therefore, comes ahead of the job, and consists of imparting the vision and the drive. Once the work starts, you need to let everyone get on with it. To micromanage the process is to risk slowing it down.

> The job of the leader is to provide the vision and then get out of the way ... When people know where to go and are doing a good job at getting there, then the only thing leadership can do is mess it up. As a leader, you have selected the best resources, set the expectation of performance, motivated the group to a greater cause and spent time developing each team member; now, go find something to do.

That, surely, is the way that head teachers should see their own teaching. They aren't doing it to demonstrate how good they are. It's important to say that, because some heads feel a bit guilty if they aren't brilliant in class, and yet that's not the point. It's perfectly possible to demonstrate good practice and sound professionalism without being awesomely inspirational, and you can argue that a head who has to work at being a good teacher, who isn't a natural, is more likely to understand what the job is really like.

Neither can it be said that the teaching head is leading from the front, because there's a very real chance that they're actually trailing behind. Once in the classroom, after all, a head becomes part of a team led by someone else – a head of department or a subject leader.

No, once the teaching day is under way, the head's leadership contribution is already in the bank, in the form of expectations, motivation, coaching and professional development. Now it's time to go and just join in. And in the course of their classroom work our heads will, like those young officers, do some learning – about themselves, their colleagues, their children, and most of all about the work done day by day in the classroom. And everyone will end up the better for it.

R. Todd Stephens PhD (2005) *Leadership in a Natural Disaster*, DMReview.com, 20 October.

You can't always achieve perfection

They say that politics is the art of the possible. Running a school's a bit like that too. You can make plans, and rules, and strategies, but you'll still end up struggling to get through the day. Suppose, for example, a child persistently turns up to school in clothes that break the uniform rules. Do you punish the child? It's probably his mum that's sent him out in the wrong shirt – and who knows what pressures she's under? But a rule's a rule, isn't it? That's certainly what the other parents are thinking when they look accusingly at you.

Bending before the wind

One day, in that galaxy far far away where I was a head teacher, a woman came up to me after our Friday morning parents' assembly to have a little moan about the girl who'd been sitting in front of her.

'She had about half a dozen earrings in each ear', she said. 'I thought you had a rule about that.'

I sighed, that special sigh that all head teachers know about, and said: 'That's right. We do have such a rule. She shouldn't be wearing them.'

'Well,' she said (and here I had to restrain myself from joining in the chorus), 'what are you going to do about it?'

'I've told her many times', I said. 'I've written to her parents. I've had them in and suggested various ways forward. Each time they've agreed, then gone away and forgotten about it. Now what do you want me to do next?'

I ran through the options with her. Wrestle the child to the ground and forcibly remove the offending baubles? Clearly not. Suspend her from school? No, the woman, a reasonable person at heart, believed with me that such a thing wouldn't be appropriate. Did she have any further suggestions? No, she didn't. So, in the end, we agreed together that provided we were successful in maintaining a good relationship with the vast majority of parents then we'd just have to deal with the others individually as best we could, without taking out our irritations on the children. Most people, after all, have been around long enough to know that life has some unfair lumps in it, which just have to be swallowed. Frankness, and a clear admission of my own fallibility, worked, as it so often did.

The word here, I suppose, is 'tolerance'.

I thought of this when a head teacher – not one from the distant past, but someone dealing with today's very real and alarming world – pointed out to me one of the many contradictions in official policy brought about by government's built-in attempts to please everyone simultaneously.

'We're urged to have, at the same time, both "full inclusion" of all children, and "zero tolerance" of all kinds of bad behaviour', he said. 'Now how exactly is that supposed to work?'

As I listened, I was reminded very much of the twin noticeboards outside a large school in one of our cities. One says: 'Somesuch Community School'. The other says: 'Keep Out'.

You learn some things very quickly

You can spend a lot of time learning the lessons of leadership – there are courses in it after all. Some of the best lessons, though, are learned quickly and hard, as the result of making mistakes.

Embarrassing moments

Once, when I was a deputy head, I was in the staffroom at break joking with colleagues when I realised that the break was well over and all the children would now be in the building. I looked around, and began to say something friendly and encouraging like:

'Well, folks, I think it's time we went to class.'

However, I got only as far as 'Well ...' when the door burst open and the head came in. He looked around, jerked his thumb towards the door and made that quick whistle between the bottom lip and the top teeth that means 'Out!'

It was a good lesson. In fact it was several lessons. I learned that as deputy I shouldn't become too comfortably ensconced not only in the staffroom but in its culture – and that when I became a head I'd be well advised to cut off from it completely. I learned that for one member of staff to be late to class is no trifling affair, but something that exposes children to physical danger, including increased opportunities for bullying. And lastly, I learned that while gentle admonition is fine, sometimes you need a bit more, in which case the thumb and the whistle come in handy. Except that I could never manage the whistle, which rather spoiled the effect.

Recalling this, I began to think of other examples of lessons learned in the same quick and salutary way.

There was that sports day, for example. I was a new head by then, and I was determined it was going to be a good fun event, with lots of parents. The deputy head got busy with charts and lists, as they do. The caretaker covered the field in a bewildering maze of ropes and posts. Teachers gathered their teams around them during the morning and gave them pep talks.

Then out we all went and there began a magnificent and brilliantly organised pageant of physical endeavour, while I walked self-importantly around in a straw hat nodding at the parents.

Then it rained. Actually it poured – suddenly, and comprehensively. And everyone, parents, children, teachers, just raced for indoors. In seconds the field was deserted, posts and ropes scattered, bits of equipment lying about, while the interior of the building was a jammed and yelling mass of very wet people. I stood there entirely helpless, mouth opening and closing. Short of firing a revolver over the heads of the crowd, like First Officer Murdoch on the *Titanic*, I couldn't think of anything to do except gradually calm things down with the help of colleagues. It was the most disorganised, unseemly few minutes I've ever seen in a primary school, and I was in charge of it. One of my young colleagues was standing near me, and I always remember him saying, both to himself and to me.

'This is appalling!' in a shocked, disbelieving voice.

And then he checked himself, because he'd realised that he was implicitly criticising me. So, bless him, he rapidly adjusted his words so as to assume a share of the responsibility.

'We are appalling!' he said, the second time.

I wasn't deceived. I knew I carried the can for the shambles. And all because I failed to ask (or even think) at the planning stage: 'What do we do if … ?'

From that moment, my deputy, a hugely practical person, had the specific job of asking the 'What do we do if … ?' questions in all planning sessions. (You can still get caught out of course, but at least the mindset's in place.)

Did you have some key learning events in your career? Of course you did. It would be good to hear about them. I asked my friend Bob, a long-serving head, about his.

'One of our teachers had been having a good parents' evening – friendly, relaxed', he recalled. 'Then the very last couple she saw verbally savaged her for no apparent reason. We talked about it, and realised together that when parents are angry it's often because they're being defensive about their own belief that they're not coping. And that sometimes if they have issues with each other, they'll deal with them by both attacking the teacher.'

That being so, he realised, there was no point, and certainly no advantage to the child, in getting into confrontation, and that building bridges with parents wasn't necessarily going to be as easy as the textbooks sometimes imply.

What can really bring you up short, though, is to look back at your career and realise that there were many events from which you failed to learn anything at all. When I was well into my headship I told a veteran head with whom I'd once worked that I was thinking of applying for a new job. In a second headship, I suggested, you can look back at the mistakes you made the first time round.

'And make them all over again!' he boomed cheerfully, smiting me on the shoulder.

Don't assume everyone thinks like you

It doesn't do to assume too readily that everything's going well, or that everyone on the team is as enthusiastic as you are, or even that they know what they're supposed to be doing. That kind of entirely unwarranted and evidence-free projection of your own knowledge, attitudes and values can lead to disillusionment and trouble.

Assumption Junction

Is everything going well in your little empire? Does everyone share your determination to see things improving? Do they spend as much time as you do thinking of what could be done better and more efficiently?

Is it yes to all of those? If so, welcome to Assumption Junction, the cosy place where the view outside the window is always restful and reassuring.

There are many, many terrible stories to be told of what can happen if the leader moves into Assumption Junction. Winston Churchill was plunged almost into despair in February 1942 because he'd wrongly assumed that Singapore was heavily fortified against the Japanese advance. (He referred repeatedly, in a phrase that many even at the time knew to be a travesty, to 'Fortress Singapore'.)

Then there's the local businessman I met a few years ago. He almost lost his thriving business because he assumed that the family members who worked for him would be honest and hard-working. They weren't. They wanted quick cash and blow the long haul, or giving good service.

And a head teacher in our county had a year of angst and distress because of her predecessor's assumption that the long-serving secretary wasn't the kind of person who would steal the dinner money. In fact she'd been doing it for years. And guess who the Chair of Governors, a vicar, chose to believe when the new head told him of her suspicions?

One of the best examples of the power of assumption was a story I came across on an online blog by a splendid person called Abi Sutherland of Edinburgh. Abi noticed something peculiar about the spiky iron fence around her workplace. On each spike – every one, over 300 in all – was a lump of discarded chewing gum. That was bizarre enough. What really got her going, though, was that one day some workmen turned up to paint the fence.

Yes, you've guessed it. They painted the lumps of gum too, first with primer, then with black enamel. And Abi posts the photographs to prove it.

'Really – who paints over a lump of chewing gum?' she asks in wonderment. 'Surely if you want the paint to stick (which is why you prime) you should remove any extraneous substances?'

Ah, the naïvety of youth. (And don't you love 'extraneous substances'?) Well, Abi, it's a good example of someone who, presumably unlike you, simply doesn't care enough about their responsibilities. A supervisor, for example, has made one of two assumptions. Either they just assumed that this was a fence like any others they'd done, and there was no need to go and look at it. Or they had looked it, seen the chewing gum, and assumed that the workforce would remove it. Had a supervisor and the worker visited the site together to discuss the job, spotted the gum and reached agreement on how to deal with it, neither of these false assumptions would have arisen.

The error here is that of projecting your own deeply held values onto a group of individuals, some of whom may share them and others of whom certainly do not.

It happens all the time, and it's easy to see why. A leader, almost by definition, is consumed by the needs of the organisation and by the drive to make it as good as it can be. Every day he or she comes in filled with plans, eager to write the memos and hold the meetings. It's so easy to forget, or never fully to realise, that not everyone in the place is like that. Some just want to do the job and go home. Others don't even want to do the job – they'll go through the motions and keep out of the way. The real skill of leadership, you might conclude, lies not in having visions and making speeches, but in knowing all of your people so well that even if you can't persuade them to share your strategic ideals, then you can get them committed to their own bit of the mission. The orchestral conductor has a broad understanding of how the symphony should sound. The second trombone may not be signed up to that, but so long as the conductor can get the player to be keen about the second trombone part, everything will be fine.

And in school? Well, there's the head, for example, who assumes that everyone is as single-mindedly fired up about the need to improve the school as she is. The belated realisation, too often, is that in truth it's not quite like that. In the real world of school, responsibilities might be shirked, meetings avoided, problems not chased down.

On the other side of the coin, there's the leader who doesn't explain everything, so that even if the staff are willing and anxious to do the right thing, they're constantly running into problems that the leader's missed through not talking things through properly in advance. How many times have you heard someone who's taken on a new role say:

'It turned out there was much more to it than she told me. I didn't like to go back to her, because I thought I was supposed to know.'

It's clarity that's needed. Look at the task together, and agree on what it is, and what needs to be done. Then open up some opportunities for feedback on how it's developing.

It's easy for us to see what the painting boss should have done – an arm round the shoulder and: 'Look Jack, it's a messy old job, but if it can be done by Friday, like you say, there's a drink in it for you. I'll pop round Wednesday and see how it's looking.'

Try it on your head of maths next time he throws the strategy document through the window.

Story of the chewing gum fence, final chapter, with links to earlier episodes: http://www.sunpig.com/abi/archives/2005/06/05/the_gum_fence_the_final_chapter/#more

Offering more work, but no more money

I suppose in any walk of life there's the phenomenon of 'false promotion'. This is where someone is given extra duties, dressed up with a fancy title, but with no extra money in sight. It certainly happens in teaching, where budgets are often tight, and heads and governors sometimes have to be creative about how they allocate responsibilities. Before being cynical about this, it's worth looking at what's to be gained.

Swallow it. It'll do you good.

There's an episode of the BBC comedy series *The Office* in which the spooky Gareth points out that he's been made a 'team leader'. Tim, the nice guy, tells him it doesn't mean anything.

'It's a title someone's given you to get you to do something they don't want to do for free – it's like making the div kid at school milk monitor. No one respects it.'

It isn't at all unknown for school leaders to create 'cash-free promotions'. I was once made, in a Birmingham comprehensive, a 'senior house tutor'. It carried some responsibilities – not nearly as many as the job title might lead you to think, because the real power resided in the heads of lower, middle and upper school. There was certainly no extra money.

As SHT I looked after inter-house sport and out-of-school activities, and ran a weekly vertically organised house assembly during which the sixth formers treated my antics with languidly amused tolerance.

I was, in fact, in a kind of hierarchical cul-de-sac, with no access to the mainstream of power and influence. It seems likely – though I wasn't aware of it at the time – that the department and phase heads regarded me and the others in my position (there were four or five of us as I recall) as irrelevant.

Eventually, though, the real value of the job was revealed when I was able to include it in job applications. It helped me to an interview for a real house head's job, on a lot more money, in a school which actually was organised in vertical houses, and where the house heads were the people who counted.

So, if you want to ask someone to take on extra work, with nothing much on offer beyond a title and the possibility of some money in the future, you could do worse than point out the advantages that I reaped from my quasi-elevation. I can think of five without trying too hard, and there may have been more.

1 I was drawn into a team of congenial and creative people. My house staff team was endless fun. The head of PE, a larger-than-life Olympic medallist, was one of them and I cherish my memories of the time I had with him.
2 My work, although apparently peripheral, did make a contribution to the life of the school. We had some good fundraising ideas and we were responsible for raising enough money to buy the school's first minibus.
3 The responsibilities looked good on my CV and on job applications.
4 The job lined up well with my curriculum responsibilities. At that time I was working with special needs children. As a senior house tutor I developed a different relationship with them and also was able to see them in the context of the school population as a whole.
5 It was a good forward step for me. It got me a job as a 'proper' house head, and from there I went on to be a middle school deputy and later a head. Being a house head was a better jumping-off point from secondary than being an academic department head.

So if, as a school leader you need to make this kind of appointment, then at least think through – and discuss with the teacher – the long-term implications. They can be positive, and you can set them out honestly and with a clear conscience.

Moving on from headship

A full teaching career is forty years. Many teachers become heads in half that time or less. And, yes, some do stay in headship for twenty or twenty-five years, retiring in their pomp, garlanded with affection and respect.

Some, though, look at the years ahead and wonder, simply, 'Is this it?'

So, what does come next? Do you settle down and wait for retirement? Or are there further steps to be taken?

Carry on Teacher

We are told that in 1918, at the end of the Great War to End all Wars, when the huge British conscript army was disbanded, lost and bewildered men queued for mundane jobs, suddenly bereft of a sense of common purpose. Richard Holmes's magnificent book *Tommy* tells us that 'It was a common sight in London to see ex-officers with barrel organs.'

Much the same happened, some years ago, to primary heads, when early retirement was an easier option than it is now. Active and assertive men and women, accustomed to commanding attention when they entered a room, suddenly discovered not only that they were ordinary mortals after all ('There is a queue here, love'), but that no matter how good the retirement deal, it still didn't pay nearly as well as a salary.

None of them, to my knowledge, turned to barrel organs – though the late and much-missed Mike Lee, once a gleeful thorn in the flesh of Warwickshire authority, played the concertina in the streets of Nuneaton, albeit for charity.

Many, of course, became providers of in-service training. For a time, on any course you attended, speaker after speaker was introduced as 'a former head teacher'. It couldn't last. Just how long can someone who's cashed in their chips go on dictating the game? Warwickshire's professional development leader at the time reckoned that the shelf life of a former head was eighteen months. That was then – it's probably about eighteen minutes now.

The underlying problem, always, has been that primary headship can go on for a long time. A head appointed before the age of forty has, in theory, a quarter of a century still to serve. For the first three to five years there will be juicy challenges – the coming of the new double glazing, the painless removal of Mr Gimcrack, the placing of a bomb under the caretaker. After that, what? All too often, sooner or later there is the arrival at a plateau which, in reality, is an imperceptible downward slope.

In any other walk of life there'd be somewhere else to go. But where? Teacher education is increasingly being done in school. Local authority professional development is, rightly, being delievered by serving heads. Another school? You've fought that battle once already, and there aren't too many who yearn to do it all over again, carrying a few more years, five kilos of extra weight and your daughter's wedding coming up.

So, unsurprisingly, there have always been many who've looked for something else to do.

At this point I should describe the exit route that I took, after eleven years of headship and an increasing feeling that it was time for somebody else to take over. In short, I put together one of those multi-task 'portfolio' jobs. Mine included some writing, some lecturing, some supply teaching and a little private keyboard tuition. A year before I left my headship, when I was pondering the options, a colleague head said to me: 'A year from now you'll be supremely happy, and wondering why you ever hesitated.'

He was, of course, absolutely right. The balance of the portfolio has changed – which is the whole point of having one of course – but every single day I still consciously stop for a moment to appreciate my good fortune. This attracts the interest of heads and teachers who wish they could do something similar to the extent that I ought to set out some words of advice.

The first thing to realise is that nobody owes you anything. Whether you want to write articles, teach on supply or deliver hilarious after-dinner speeches, what you offer must be in tune with what the buyer needs. A supply teacher, even a former head, cannot be a visiting celebrity, cosseted by the rest of the staff. A writer of articles must provide material that fits the publication in every possible way – length, style, subject. Working in the public sector for years tends to make you forget these things.

That in turn leads on to the next rule, which is that you have to start preparing for your new life long before you leave the old one. In your last year particularly you should observe the old naval principle of 'One hand for the ship and one hand for yourself'. If that means taking the odd day off to pursue contacts and opportunities, then so be it. You've surely given enough over the years.

Then, take advice about money – whether to take your pension, what to do with a lump sum, whether to start a new pension. I made mistakes in that area, which I cannot now rectify and which I could have avoided had I talked well in advance to professionals, including my union, about my plans.

Finally, be open-minded. I know former heads who work happily delivering new cars right across the UK. Heads delivering cars? Think about it – if you had to send a new car from Basingstoke to Glasgow, would you rather it was driven by a twenty-year-old from the Job Centre or a fifty-five-year-old respectable head teacher? (Yes, I know. Just keep the thought to yourself.)

Managing an impossible staff member

If there's one single problem that can blight the life of a head teacher it's having an inadequate caretaker or site manager. The wrong person can wreak havoc in ways that belie his or her apparently modest status in the hierarchy. Such people undoubtedly exist, and they're usually clever enough to avoid formal disciplinary action. Here's a story about how one head tackled the caretaker from hell.

The caretaker from hell

A primary school appointed a new caretaker. Although he'd not done that kind of work before – which is quite common – he came with good references, and was well known to some of the governors as a local handyman and generally helpful soul.

Before long, it became apparent that he was a disaster. He was manipulative, sly and dishonest. The good impression he'd made on people before he came, and during his interview, was a carefully constructed front. He did the absolute minimum of official work, preferring to do high-profile favours for teachers and governors. Then he spent ages whingeing to the head about the obstacles preventing him from doing a good job.

The head, accustomed through her career to caretakers who were willing, open-hearted genuine friends of their schools, was at her wits' end wondering what to do. She was being put on the back foot by a person the likes of whom she'd never had to deal with before, yet who was essential to the running of the school.

'You're the head', she said to herself. 'How can a caretaker get you stressed like this?'

What was needed, the head felt, was a confrontation, perhaps a formal disciplinary warning. The case though would be very tenuous. The work was being done, albeit to a minimum standard, and trying to force the issue might well end with the caretaker, supported by his union, coming out best and now well entrenched.

It was the head's American-born elderly mum who had the best advice in the end.

'I guess it's time', she said, 'to put the dog on the porch.'

That phrase, she explained, originated in Texas where, if a dog was ill-behaved, you didn't have a battle ('BAD dog!' Thwack!) – you put the miscreant out on the porch, put food out from time to time, got on with life and waited to see what happened.

'Don't talk with the guy any more than you have to', said her mother. 'Leave him written instructions and don't get into arguments. Be the cold and distant boss. Then wait him out.'

So that's what our head did, and as soon as the decision was made, she immediately felt freed from the burden of uncertainty. She was relentlessly polite, correct, cool and direct, avoiding discussion, failing to respond to gossip, playing everything by the book.

Within a year, the caretaker was gone, seeking someone else to manipulate. The dog, starved of attention, had fled the porch.

Don't use the school to indulge your personal skills

When you're the boss, you have the opportunity to pick and choose the activities and jobs that you really enjoy. But this can lead you into self-indulgence, and neglect of your key responsibilities.

Look at me everybody!

I made many mistakes as a head, but maybe the longest-lasting was to take to myself the running of the school choir.

I took every child who wanted to come and we met just about every day, at morning break, because I believed then – and still do – that for primary music groups a short session every day is much better than a long rehearsal every week. For me, that rehearsal spot was sacrosanct. I'd walk out of whatever I was doing to meet my choir in the hall at 10.15. I put in a lot of preparation time, too, finding and arranging music, and making arrangements for concerts and trips.

It all paid off. We had a great choir, though I say it as shouldn't. We won competitions, we graced municipal occasions, we made the Royal Festival Hall, and we supported big adult choirs at major concerts.

I was sure the benefits both to the children, who were given pride and confidence, and to the school as a whole were far-reaching, and that this was a particular talent of mine that I should use. I recall the occasion when we did a concert with a very accomplished adult choir – the Reading Phoenix in fact. Afterwards, two of the Reading members came up to me and spoke in glowing terms about the way our children were being given confidence and pride.

But at the same time I always wondered whether it was taking up too much of my time and attention. It's significant that not long ago I said as much to a friend, a former colleague, and instead of offering the reassurance I was after, he just smiled and nodded. It offered just a hint – which

I shrank from pursuing – of what he and the others were thinking and saying at the time.

There were so many other things to do, after all. Too many for the head to be so deeply involved in one activity. It wasn't as if we didn't have a music specialist either, for we had a great teacher who, I now believe, could have run the choir in her own way with proper management support from me.

What we're talking about here, of course, is delegation. Someone once compared delegation with going through your wardrobe with a view to thinning it out. You take out a garment and it's something you really like, and would like to hang on to, but really you know that it would look even better on somebody else. And in any case, it no longer fits the image you want to portray.

I think of it this way. At the schools prom, what's the proper place to find a head teacher? On the stage in a white tux? Or in the audience, surrounded by supporters, colleagues, friends, avuncular, dewy-eyed and bursting with pride?

The friend I mentioned earlier, having learned the teaching trade with me, went on to headship. His school, too, developed a speciality akin to my choir. In their case it was a nationally known Bhangra dancing group. My friend supported it tirelessly. But he didn't teach Bhangra, or spend much time at the rehearsals. That he left to a specialist who could give herself wholeheartedly with a clear conscience.

It was an object lesson in leadership. My friend was a huge enthusiast for the Bhangra dancers, talking about them, following them to events and, crucially, using his management expertise and depth of experience to assure the group's continuing development. Positioned as he was, he was also able to encourage across the whole school and the community an enthusiasm for the Bhangra group that I couldn't achieve with my choir, which was never really 'owned' by anyone but me.

(I could hardly, after all, stand up in assembly and offer fulsome praise to my choir and to its leader, my good self.)

In the case of the Bhangra group it was important, as in all delegation, that both of the people in the equation were clear about the strategic aim. In this case it was to develop an excellent open-access activity that would be enjoyable and educative for the children involved and would widely promote the school's values of inclusion and commitment to the arts.

It all adds up to the fact that delegation doesn't mean handing a task over and then forgetting about it. That's more like abdication. One of the clearest statements of this comes from Indian business leader P.S. Rao, who says, on the 'Hindu Businessline' website:

Delegation is not simply an attitude; it is a planned developmental activity. Different people require different levels of delegation, and the same people also require different levels of delegation on different tasks. Verbalise it, plan it, gradually develop people from one level to another. Delegation is a commitment to oneself.

www.thehindubusinessline.com

Spreading the concept of leadership

We tend to think of organisations as having a leader – or a leadership team – at the top, with everyone else following on behind. Increasingly, though, we're hearing of the concept of 'distributed leadership'. It's not difficult to see that that might mean delegation to a middle level, but true distributed leadership goes further than that, and envisages an organisation in which everyone takes leadership of their own area of work. In the article which inspired this column, management writer Brent Filson explains what this means to him.

Pride in the job

A train of thought led me recently to look at some job descriptions on the web for school cleaners. I was amazed by the detail in some of them. One, for example, for a part-time cleaner, was two pages long, beginning with: 'The cleaner will be required to safeguard and promote the welfare of children and young people.'

The long list then continues. It includes, as well as the expected technical stuff, 'to work as part of a team of maintenance staff and contribute to the overall ethos, aims and work of the school, by fostering and facilitating good relationships between staff'.

And, 'to participate in training, other learning activities and professional development as required'.

The person specification continues the theme by asking for attributes which include 'the ability to recognise areas in need of improvement' and 'the ability to plan, organize and prioritize'.

Now it would be easy to look askance at all of this and say:

'Come on! It's a cleaning job, for Heaven's sake.'

But no. Here's an advert and a job description that send some very clear signals. This is a school that's serious about its recruitment at every level, is proud of the way all of the staff are signed up to its core mission, and is anxious that new recruits realise that. What's wanted isn't just someone who glumly pushes a mop, but a person who can become a resourceful and committed leader of their part of the school's work.

I turned to that, and other job descriptions, after reading an article, on Buzzle.com, by management writer Brent Filson on how leaders know that they're being successful. At least as important an indicator as measured results, he writes, is the degree to which the people being led are themselves leaders. Leaders, he suggests, don't just do the job.

'There's a crucial difference between doing a task and taking leadership of that task that makes a world of difference in the task's accomplishment', he writes. 'For instance, if one is a floor sweeper, doesn't one best accomplish one's task not simply by doing floor sweeping but by taking leadership of floor sweeping?'

He goes on to explain what this means – showing initiative, setting personal goals, evaluating results, creating an 'esprit'.

(We've all had cleaners like that of course – going the extra mile every day, watchful of the children's welfare, openly proud of the school and their very visible contribution to it.)

That works, of course, at every level. If top leadership is excellent, then everyone, TA, class teacher, subject or year head, will be a leader of his or her own bit of the enterprise – ahead of the game, trying new things, measuring effects, bringing people along, taking pride in being part of the whole.

'Whenever you need to lead people to accomplish a task,' writes Filson, 'challenge them not to do that task but to take leadership of that task.'

It's a brave thing to do of course. It means letting go, in an atmosphere of great confidence and, above all, trust on all sides. Filson's argument, though, is that when it works – when everyone in the organisation is working effectively in leadership mode, then that's the best possible indicator of the effectiveness of the people at the top. He concludes: 'Your leadership should best be measured not by your leadership but by the leadership of the people you lead.'

www.buzzle.com/editorials/5-26-2005-70566.asp

Leadership in the classroom

When you analyse what happens in a school, you realise the job of running a classroom is a high-level management activity. It involves the management of people, resources and time – juggling all those elements continuously, under pressure. That's what I was trying to put across in this piece.

Keeping the plates spinning

Here's a picture of an inspirational manager and leader, a person on top form. Chris – that's this person's name – leads a demanding group of people, all different, all full of sparkle and creativity, and yet constantly demanding to be fed with more and more ideas. As Chris briefs one person, engaging in discussion, feeding in suggestions, corrections and instructions, another one has completed the last assignment and is demanding attention, wanting the job signed off and a new one allocated. Skills and abilities within the group are widely spread, and Chris has to bear this in mind all the time if the whole enterprise is to move forward smoothly.

Chris has well developed presentation skills, and an enviable ability to keep the group interested when they're called together for a briefing. Information technology obviously helps here, but the core skill of being able to engage with people – each at his or her own level, drawing out ideas, bouncing questions and answers to and fro – is what really counts.

The whole process adds up to a permanent adrenaline rush as Chris draws deeply on skill and experience to stay ahead of these lively, often eccentric individuals.

One of the biggest headaches for Chris is keeping on top of the constant demand for resources. This is an area where there is good support – there's a small team helping to feed in materials and keep them stocked up – but it's Chris's job to think ahead about strategic requirements, always bearing in mind the restrictions of a fixed budget.

Along with that goes a particularly precise need for good time management. Many tasks are run to a closely defined timetable, with little opportunity for over-runs or missed deadlines.

The planning demands, obviously, are daunting. Much of it takes place on the hoof, in response to immediate needs. That's not nearly enough, though. Strategy – long-, medium-, and short-term – has to be set out clearly, in line with the overall aims of the organisation, and this is work done in the twilight hours when the group members have gone off to their families – it's simply not possible to think and plan and do paperwork when they're around, for they soon grow impatient if there seems to be nothing to do.

It's a work hard, play hard, way of life. Chris shares sport with the group, for example. They enjoy a regional version of baseball, and various competitive games akin to paintball, but more sophisticated in that they're designed to develop skills progressively and to be played indoors or out, without the need for expensive specialised equipment or protective clothing.

Chris also takes the group on awaydays, where there are opportunities to relax and eat together, perhaps enjoying some mental stimulation in a museum or heritage centre.

To experience Chris at work is to see a true leader in action – each member of the group genuinely wants to do well and receive praise. Each one, too, makes visible and gratifying progress as Chris gives coaching and guidance that's carefully judged to be appropriately gentle or assertive. There are crises, of course – tantrums, even, for if you put such a diverse group together, each member demanding lots of attention, and all different in the way they tackle their work, then you're bound to have some nervy moments. The danger is, of course, that the most demanding members of the group attract more attention, and perhaps more resources, and this is something that Chris has to guard against and take account of in the planning process.

But enough of this, because you're well ahead of me. This isn't Chris the leader of a creative group in an advertising agency, or of a roomful of young turks in the financial sector. This is Christine, any reception teacher in any school in the land.

But let's not just smile smugly and leave it there. We need to remember that every head teacher has the task of leading a whole team of people like Chris – and that, clearly, calls for some very special qualities. In 2000, the Hay Group compared 200 head teachers with 200 business leaders, and came to a conclusion that's been regularly and proudly trotted out ever since: 'the role of headteacher is stretching by comparison to business. Even highly successful executives would struggle to exert outstanding leadership in schools.'

What's not so often quoted is the bit that says there are areas for improvement. Among them is the conclusion that 'Headteachers rely too heavily on telling people what to do.'

Very clearly, Chris and her colleagues won't necessarily thrive best in a regime where they're told what to do. Leading such people is altogether more subtle and difficult. There are many quotations and statements that sum this up. Here's one I like, from *Managing the Professional Service Firm* by David H. Maister:

> Leaders are needed to be the guardians of the long term. They are valuable when they act as the conscience of their colleagues: not necessarily giving them new goals, but helping them achieve the goals they have set for themselves.

www.haygroup.co.uk/Expertise/downloads/The_Lessons_of_Leadership.pdf
David H. Maister (1997) *Managing the Professional Service Firm*, New York: Simon & Schuster.

The staffroom tells a story about the school

Every school has a staffroom, or something that does the same job. The state of it, whether it's heavily used or not, the facilities in there, can tell you a lot about the health of a school and, particularly, about what the leadership's attitude is to the care and well-being of the workforce. It's a theme I've returned to several times over the years. Here, I'm moved to return to it by a discussion I found on the TES *'staffroom' website forum.*

Private sanctuary

What do you think your staffroom's for? Is it a private place where teachers can 'let off steam'? I ask because that particular phrase 'let off steam' was used quite a lot in a recent exchange on a teachers' chatroom. The topic under discussion was about how a member of the senior team should handle an overheard insulting tirade directed at the head (who wasn't there of course).

That 'private sanctuary' idea used to be very common. Taken to its extreme, you get what I found in the long-ago demolished Tilton Road Primary in Birmingham. There, the handful of men on the staff, tired of mixing with the women, had built themselves a private male staffroom by boxing in the landing on top of a fire escape with reclaimed chipboard, and equipping it with exactly the kind of second-hand furniture that you'd expect of any group of grumpy old men (of whatever age). There, they could smoke, reminisce about a lost golden age and generally whinge away to their hearts' content. One of them, I recall, had a hoard of contraband cigarettes which he sold from an old desk. And down the corridor the women had their own staffroom – actually it was the real staffroom where they did their own brand of whingeing and reminiscing in rather more civilised surroundings.

It didn't take long for that sort of segregation to die out. The 'sanctuary' idea, though, lingered on for many years. You'd find staffrooms from which all support staff were excluded. (People outside education found that difficult to take. I remember going to a conference in the nineties and hearing a business executive accusing teachers of being the most class-conscious working group he'd ever come across.)

Commonly, too, there'd be a notice saying: 'Pupils are not to knock on this door.'

Things are different now, though, surely? The staffroom can't be any sort of private den, whether single-sex or mixed – too many people have access to it. A few weeks ago I spent an hour or so sitting in the staffroom of a primary, waiting for a particular teacher to become free. During that time a steady stream of people popped in and out. All of them spoke to me. Not one of them, as far as I could tell, was a teacher. There were administrators, teaching assistants, parent-volunteers, lunchtime supervisors. Schools are like that now. It's increasingly rare to find that teachers make up the majority of the workforce.

What's certainly true though – and it's up to experienced colleagues to set the pace here – is that teachers are, by definition and by qualification, the leading professionals in the school. They're the people to whom all the other groups look for professional leadership – which includes how to behave in the staffroom. And professional staffroom behaviour includes not making unwise broadcast remarks and judgements about individual parents, children or colleagues.

I think I've used the phrase 'proudly a teacher' before. I make no apology, because the words resonate with me. They were used by a head teacher friend to describe, at his funeral, a dear colleague who died, far too early, in harness. 'Proudly a teacher', for me, implies behaving like one.

Are you a different person at home?

We assume we present different faces to our various audiences – that we're not the same at home as we are at work, for example. In one of the many Second World War histories I've read, there's a photograph of Air Marshal 'Bomber' Harris – usually portrayed as stern, even ruthless – playing in his garden with his children. A different person at home, you're meant to think. And yet, when you look, he's still in his uniform, rank insignia, medals and all.

Not at school now

Hand on heart, now, has anyone at home ever said to you something like:
    'Don't talk to me like that. You're not at school now!'
    I guess they probably have. It's certainly happened to me lots, and it makes me wonder two things.
    First, does it happen to people in other jobs?
    'Don't be sarky with me, you're not answering PM's Questions now.'
    (Actually, you know that one almost certainly happens, don't you?)
    Really, though, I suppose what we're asking is whether when you're at home you're a different person from the one at work? I thought a lot about this after I'd seen the excellent Timothy Spall as Albert Pierrepoint, Britain's official hangman, in the biographical film *Pierrepoint*. He certainly left his job behind when he came home. Or rather he left himself behind when he went into the condemned cell.
    'When I go in there, I leave Albert Pierrepoint outside', he says.
    On the face of it, it seems inevitable that anyone in any kind of responsible position, and not just the national hangman, is going to act differently at home. In fact there's jokey mileage to be had from assuming this not to be the case – think of Captain von Trapp in *The Sound of Music*, parading his children to the blasts of a whistle. No, home is

where the feared and austere professional loosens the waistband, kicks off the shoes and becomes a pussycat.

But what are we really saying here? That you really and truly are two different people, one at work, one at home? And maybe a third in some other setting – at your sports club or in the choir? It's not like that surely. All you're actually doing is simply obeying the rules and conventions of whichever setting you're in. All that's on the surface. You have one set of rules and conventions for yourself at home, another set for work, and yet others for the school, the pub, the club or whatever. Underneath, in the core of your personality, you're the same person. To try to change that, to be something you're not, is no way to run your life. It's too difficult to keep it up, for one thing (the story of *Pierrepoint* is of exactly that pressure).

I suppose teachers, maybe more than most people, have to adopt a persona when they're at work in the classroom. Even there, though, it's not a real change of personality. Were you really to try to become someone different, you'd find that the people who matter – the children – are astonishingly good at knowing what you're trying to do. So in the end, though you may do some play-acting, and make some changes in the way you speak and behave, in the end you can only be yourself.

Stanford University Professors Jeffrey Pfeffer and Robert I. Sutton make the point very well in their excellent myth-busting book, *Hard Facts, Dangerous Half-Truths and Total Nonsense*. They have a chapter called 'Is work fundamentally different from the rest of life and should it be?': 'it takes lots of effort and emotional energy to leave one's essential nature at the workplace door ... And it is simply impossible for many of the best people to stifle their true selves.'

Among the stories they tell is that of Libby Sartain, a top internet executive in the USA who in her early years was constantly causing unease by being cheerful at work. She was actually turned down for one job for smiling too much, and she left another after her boss said to her:

> You're so much fun to be around and I really enjoy working with you. But when you laugh out loud in the hall, people are going to think you're not very professional. You need to tone it down a little bit.

Many, perhaps most, organisations are like that, they say – they assume that it's right to be a different sort of person at work. The trouble is, they argue, it's a line of thought that leads to false assumptions – that, for example, people need different sorts of motivation at work than they do at home – money and incentives at work, obligations to others and joy in achievement at home.

Good organisations, they conclude, accept people for who they are, and build on their strengths. So don't worry – if you're doing the job, supporting your team, challenging your pupils, just go with being the person you are. And, it goes without saying, remember that the same principle of acceptance applies in your dealings with your colleagues, your pupils and their families.

Jeffrey Pfeffer and Robert I. Sutton (2006) *Hard Facts, Dangerous Half-Truths and Total Nonsense: Profiting from Evidence-Based Management*, Boston, Mass: Harvard Business School Press.

Keeping ahead of the job

Do you know there's a thing called 'flow'? It's a sort of emotional and mental state in which everything's going right and you feel that you can't put a foot wrong. Sportsmen and women obviously recognise something like that, and it may well be recognisable in every other walk of life. If that's so – if you can attain the state of 'flow' as a teacher or a head – then perhaps the long summer holiday is a real mistake, because you just have to get back into the magical state when you come back. That's the argument here anyway. Or perhaps, in truth, I was just attracted by the name of the psychologist who first described the phenomenon.

Flow

Remember the Vulcan Bomber? A wonderful machine, a great four-engined delta-winged jet, part of the 'V force' that carried our nuclear deterrent in the late fifties through into the seventies. Most of the time, when they started it up, they did it like your holiday jet – fire up one engine at a time until all four are idling.

Some of the aircraft, though, were kept bombed and fuelled up, ready to be in the air before the Russian missiles arrived. (The government said we'd get four minutes. The jokes about what to do during those minutes still go the rounds.) Those Quick Reaction Alert aircraft had to have all four engines blasted into action simultaneously – a 'four-engine start'. And we're not talking about modern quiet bypass motors here. These were your actual Concorde-style Bristol Olympus engines. No one who saw and heard this Götterdämmerung, uniquely awesome, procedure will ever forget the experience.

Well, if you're a teacher or a head, coming back to school after a long holiday can be a bit like a four-engine start. At the beginning of the holiday you went through the process that's always called 'winding down'. Your brain, heartbeat and emotional state stay at their peak for a while, and then very gradually slow down, power off, turbine gradually whining to a standstill.

When the holiday's over, though, there's no winding up. There's the full, in-your-face experience right from the start, even though everything inside you is going,

'Hang on! Let's just get the feel of things first!'

The trouble is, you really can't pick up the pace just like that. Even Pavlov's dogs, we're told (remember them?), had to be taught the whole salivating thing over again if they had a long break.

The message for school leaders is obvious – stay out of the loop for too long and it's going to be difficult to get back into it.

What you're trying to regain, against all the odds, given the multiple start-of-term irritations, is what another psychologist, Dr Mihaly ('Mike') Csikszentmihalyi, formerly professor of psychology at the University of Chicago, calls, simply, 'flow'. According to Professor Mike, flow is a Zen-like sense of being utterly involved in your work – ecstatic, timeless, serene. When you're in the flow, says the professor, 'The ego falls away. Time flies. Every action, movement, and thought follows inevitably from the previous one, like playing jazz.'

Many parts of the business community, including Toyota and Microsoft, have flirted with Csikszentmihalyi's ideas. Leaders at Scandinavian transport firm Green Cargo searched for 'flow' by making managers spend lots more time just talking to their people, one to one in a relaxed way – ninety minutes each, six times a year was the target.

And in school? Well, you may well have been in 'flow' last July – feeling, as you effortlessly suspended three pupils for torching the bike sheds, as if you were adding an inspired trombone riff to a Charlie Parker solo. You lost it over the holiday, though, and in September, burned by the sun, hoarse from karaoke, you're back to the National Strategies and the eternal autumn term question of where you're going for the staff Christmas dinner. It could certainly take a long time to get back into the Zone. (Yes, it's sometimes called that, too.)

I like the idea of those one-to-one sessions, though. An hour-and-a-half per teacher, with a senior colleague every half term is what it would mean in school. Impossible to find the time? That's what the Green Cargo managers said, but they did it, and performance improved all round.

Csikszentmihalyi has written many books. *Flow*, published as a paperback by Rider, is a good starting point.

Mihaly Csikszentmihalyi (2002) *Flow: The Classic Work on How to Achieve Happiness*, London: Rider.

Maybe it's the system that's wrong

Sometimes, try as you might, you can't seem to make things any better. You blame yourself, but perhaps it's not you at all. Maybe the system you're working within just isn't capable of doing what you're asking of it.

A game of marbles

The American management guru W. Edwards Deming (1900–1993), the statistician who became the brains behind Japan's industrial upsurge in the fifties, would call up members of his lecture audiences and set them to work on little experiments. Here's one you can try – your children will like it too, and there are obvious curriculum links. It would make a good science investigation for example. You need a funnel, a moveable clamp to hold it, a marble small enough to go through the funnel, a table with a white cloth and a felt-tip pen.

With the pen you draw a target on the cloth. Then you drop the marble through the funnel a number of times. Your aim is to group your hits as closely as possible around the centre of the target.

On the first try, the marble probably misses the centre. That's fine, it's what you expected. So you mark where it landed and estimate where to move the funnel to compensate. You adjust the funnel, get another marble and drop it through, expecting that you'll be a bit nearer this time. And perhaps you will. It's equally likely, though, that you'll be further away. And over a series of drops of the marble, as you persevere with moving the funnel to correct for the errors, the more you'll see your hits wandering off. And, if it were one of his lectures, Deming, in the role of manager, would castigate you for your ineptitude ('Come on, do something! Move the funnel!') to the delight of your fellow audience members.

Deming's point is that the errors have nothing to do with you. Try as you might, fiddling with the funnel won't give you a close group. The problem lies with the system, which just isn't good enough to deliver consistency from one marble drop to the next.

Another of Deming's games involves sorting red beads from white ones with the aid of a paddle perforated with holes to hold a fixed number of beads. You dip the paddle into a mixture of white and red, and your aim is to come up with a majority of white beads. There seem to be rules and skills – you're told to hold the paddle at thirty degrees for example – but in the end the result is outside the control of the operator. A super video of the red bead game in action (www.redbead.com) shows people being alternately berated or praised for differences of performance that are actually outside of their control. The message – that it's quite possible to be in a workplace where your performance will be judged against criteria that are actually outside your control – has a clarity that's actually quite scary.

What does this have to do with the task of leading our teachers? Well, imagine observing a young teacher and concluding that some lessons are good, some are satisfactory and some are terrible. How often might we shake our heads and urge her to adjust her approach, like Deming ordering his subject to shift the funnel?

On reflection, however, we might conclude that factors that are our responsibility rather than hers – planning regimes, mentoring, behaviour policy, subject leadership – are so loosely constructed that she's never going to hit the target reliably.

Obviously there'll be times when she does a wonderful lesson. She'll delight herself and think:

'OK, then – so that's how it's done!'

But then she'll find that despite a huge effort to repeat the trick, the next lesson is inexplicably even worse than before. (Come on, you know that's a familiar story. Just read the *TES* 'staffroom' postings.)

She is a living example of the key Deming message, beautifully illustrated by the funnel experiment, and by the red beads. It is that very many people – certainly more than most management teams think – work hard trying to achieve targets that are beyond their control.

'We are being ruined by best efforts', he said.

Deming's work is always rewarding to study. His approach was in many ways the antithesis of the hard-nosed management methods that had ruled American industry through the thirties and beyond, which can still be found today. He didn't believe in inspection, for example – arguing that the aim should be to build quality into the product all the way through from the beginning rather than enforce it by punitive inspection at the end. (Ring any bells, does it?)

For similar reasons he was wary of crude statistical targets. Really, what he was looking for in any institution was high quality based on pride, freedom from fear and effective leadership, rather than on penalties and targets. In particular he believed that raw targets lead to manipulation of the process so as to achieve them, and cause conflict between people and institutions who should be working together. In any case, as his 'games' were intended to demonstrate, most of the causes of low quality lie outside the control of the individuals who are striving to achieve their targets.

Deming's work was always directed at industry, and particularly at engineering, where quality is directly observable and measurable, and where it's relatively easy to see how his ideas can be applied. Education is a bit different, but nevertheless there are schools where his ideas have been taken on board. In the USA – and in this country, some individual head teachers have studied Deming and applied his principles to their work – striving for total quality throughout and starting from the principle that most people come to work wanting to do their best. If you have doubts about the value of externally imposed targets, or about inspection as a driver of school improvement, then you'll find valuable and powerful support in Deming's writings and in the work of those who follow his ideas.

www.deming.org
UK site is www.deming.org.uk

What sort of manager are you?

America's love affair with the business ethic throws up some interesting and innovative ideas – and some unusual combinations of skills. Or perhaps this is just another example of my fascination for unusual names.

Jeff's menagerie

We all know that America's a different place. As I discovered recently, for example, they don't seem to be familiar with the slow foxtrot, standing back aghast when they saw it performed by me and my wife. The full realisation of the cultural divide didn't really sink in, though, until the musical director of a high school choir tried to sell me a pair of shoes.

The choir, which was very good, was performing in the open air one summer evening in a small town in the Mid-West. At that time I had a young choir of my own, so during the interval I introduced myself to the director, who seemed pleased to see me, and asked me to come and see him later for a longer talk.

At the end of the concert he approached me bearing not, as I thought, sheets of music and curricular material, but mail order brochures for shoes. Not only did he want me to buy some, but he proposed to set me up as his UK representative. It was a bizarre experience, quite surreal in a way, and a sharp reminder that our two countries are culturally much further apart than our common language leads us to believe.

I thought of him when I came across the work of an American leadership consultant with the splendid and deeply comforting neo-Dickensian name of Jeff Earlywine. (You all smiled, didn't you? And I bet at least some of you are thinking of adopting it as a middle name.)

Jeff is much like that choral director, in that he's also an example of American's all-embracing acceptance of the business ethic. He is, in fact, a minister of religion who doubles as a consultant.

I am in no position to comment on Jeff's theology. His thoughts on leadership, though, are as clear as any I've come across. He's very good, for example, on leadership types – a subject which has generated its share of pseudo-psychological balderdash over the years.

He takes four types – maybe he invented them, but I suspect not – the lion, the beaver, the golden retriever and the otter. The reason I like them is that without any hesitation I can think of at least one real head teacher who fits each of them, and together they demonstrate just how many ways there are of succeeding in school leadership.

The lion, as you'd expect, is very visibly in the driving seat, full of confidence, strong and scary. This is the head I worked with once in Birmingham, who famously sent a teacher home to change his loud tie for something more seemly, the kind of person of whom people frequently said: 'At least you know where you are with him.' And you certainly did. Out of the door in fact if you weren't careful. But, like many lions in literature, he was possessed of a degree of compassion and understanding that often surprised. He always liked me anyway. I guess that in an earlier life I must have removed a thorn from his paw.

The beaver is the irritating perfectionist. This is the head I knew who would go round in the evening examining classroom wall displays, taking down the ones that didn't come up to scratch and leaving them spread across the teachers' desks. But who would always get everyone successfully through the day, and whose little sayings and detailed habits live on in the people she trained and are now heads themselves.

The golden retriever is peaceful, compassionate and deeply understanding. The person I think of was a nun – and before you leap in, no, I do not think that all nuns are like this. This one, though, was calm and reassuring. Her room was restfully furnished, with soft chairs, and toys for visiting toddlers, not a bit like a convent cell. Furious and spitting urban children went to her and came away fixated on heaven, like King's College choirboys. And it wasn't because she was detached from the world. On the contrary, it was more that after years as a missionary sister in the inner city, nothing would ever surprise or flummox her again.

The otter is the fun-loving, gambolling head who's surrounded by a family of like-minded people. This is the head I know in the West Midlands, whose school is filled with music, drama and dance, who always has time for you, and whose telephone voice is always on the edge of breaking into laughter. At the same time, you know there's strength and skill and pace there – how else would anyone succeed so brilliantly in a challenging environment?

Maybe you're none of these. Perhaps you're something else – a kangaroo, hopping wildly along and then getting hit by a truck. A duck-billed platypus, neither one thing nor the other. A boa constrictor, squeezing the life out of people then swallowing them whole. Never mind, you can always sell shoes.

Get the details right

In any organisation it's clearly right for the leadership to focus on the core activities. But it's a mistake to think that the peripheral details can be left to take care of themselves.

Little things mean a lot

I queued for an hotel lift recently, in the company of a large number of grey-pound coach travellers. They were weary and keen to get to their rooms. The lifts, though, were entirely inadequate for the task and some people waited a very long time with their luggage. So, in this good hotel – excellent food, friendly staff, nice rooms – what do you think was the main thing these guests were still talking about two days later?

It was a fine example of how easily an excellent organisation can be let down by a small detail. It's an issue that management guru Tom Peters tackles in his 1987 book, *Thriving on Chaos*. He once owned, he tells us, a General Motors pick-up truck.

'Nothing major has gone wrong with it', he writes. 'No dropped transmission or oil leaks. In fact it's worse than that. About eight little things have gone wrong.'

As far as he's concerned, the truck's basic reliability is entirely undermined by the stream of small problems.

> ... each time I get in the truck, it's as if a brightly lit map of GM's failure to attend to detail flashes before my eyes. Frankly, in terms of my perceptions, GM would have been better off if the transmission had failed. I would have gotten it fixed immediately, it would have been done with.

Tom's point is that so many businesses are like that – they have excellence at the heart, but it's compromised by nonsense at the periphery – poor packaging perhaps, or an incompetent help desk. In other words, the quality of what you provide isn't a matter of what you say or think it is. It's what the customer perceives it to be.

Schools are no different from businesses here. Their main concern, necessarily, and increasingly, is with the core functions of teaching and learning. As a result, we now have lots of heartening stories of schools where, by intense effort focused at the point where the teacher and the pupil meet, results have improved year on year.

Is that, though, how the customer – parent or child – perceives quality in a school? Certainly the government thinks it is, which is why we have league tables.

Me, though, I'm not so sure. Tom Peters wrote of eight little things that went wrong with his truck, and you could, I believe, put together a similar list of niggles for many schools. Here's one family's experiences, then – fictional, but only in the sense of being drawn from various sources. It's also compressed in time. But it gives the flavour, and I think it's recognisable.

> Monday. Darren goes to get his packed lunch. His chocolate bar's gone. It's a common occurrence, well known among the parents, who all think they know who does it. The school seems unable to get on top of the problem, which festers on.
>
> Tuesday. Dad snatches ten minutes from work to phone the school about the lunch box problem, but fails, in the time available, to navigate the automatic phone system. 'If you know the extension you require …' He doesn't know the extension, waits patiently through the menu but fails to raise anyone with any influence or who seems interested.
>
> Wednesday. Gran picks up the lunchbox problem. At school, she queues behind six children who are signing in late, then has trouble bending to the low reception window to speak to the receptionist, who's also fielding phone calls. She's told to take a seat. Several very preoccupied adults hurry by her without a glance.
>
> Thursday. Darren brings home a letter about a school trip that costs the thick end of £200. 'Please, Dad. All my lot are going.'
>
> Friday. Darren brings a newsletter which celebrates the school's excellent Ofsted report. 'This is a very good school …'

Yes, I know it's so easy to go on like this. Yes, it's impossible to miss all the pitfalls. Resources are stretched, and the focus has to be in the classroom. We've all, hand on heart, let things slip, upset people, ridden roughshod over concerns, momentarily forgotten that each of our pupils is the whole world to one family.

By the same token, though, perhaps we shouldn't complain if judgements are made about us on criteria that we haven't thought of and wouldn't have chosen.

Tom Peters (1987) *Thriving on Chaos: Handbook for a Management Revolution*, London: Pan.

The man who invented management

We're rightly cautious about management gurus, wondering what they have to say to us that might be of practical use in the cut and thrust of school life. We ought not to be dismissive, though, because if you listen to, or read, the right ones, you can find real wisdom. One of the first of the breed was Peter Drucker, whose key work, The Practice of Management, *was first published in 1955.*

All managers now

The pit in our village had a manager, Mr Jackson – known simply in his absence as 'Jackson' or 't'manager'. I have no idea what his Christian name was. All the kids were frightened of him. We were even frightened of his house. Pit managers were hard nuts, you see, ready to don the helmet and go down to sort the men out if necessary.

The Co-op had a manager, too – a kind smiling man in a suit, whose business was sacks of flour and sides of bacon. And our school had a headmaster – Mr Simpson, who'd served in the Far East and now enjoyed peace and freedom so much that at the slightest provocation he'd take us all out to play idyllically on the field. (How much we learned from teachers of that generation, and how missed they are now.)

By no stretch of the imagination did anyone think of these three as having anything in common in their working lives. The idea that all of them were managers, and might have had what we now call 'shared issues' to discuss was, I'm certain, never in anyone's mind.

I was moved to think of them by reading of the death of management guru Peter Drucker, who went to the Big Boardroom in November 2005, days before his ninety-sixth birthday.

Drucker, arguably, invented management, in the sense of a separate set of skills and attributes – 'Managing as specific work, and being a manager as a distinct responsibility', as he described it in the forties.

It was surely the spread of his ideas that led eventually to many people being labelled as 'managers' who had not previously been thought of like that – such as, of course, head teachers, heads of department and the like.

'Do they think I'm a biscuit factory?' we spluttered when we first heard the word. 'What's all this got to do with education?'

Now, just about everyone in school is a manager, and some have had to be promoted to the rank of 'leader', presumably in order to distinguish them from the rest.

All of that's fine, as long as we don't forget some of the principles that Drucker stood for, and which he spoke about right up to the end of his life. On his ninety-fifth birthday, in 2004, he gave an interview in which he said:

'Successful leaders don't start out asking "what do I want to do?" They ask: "what needs to be done?" Then they ask, "of those things that would make a difference, which are right for me?"'

Now that sounds simple enough when you think about it. And yet how many leaders find it difficult? How many heads have you met who start the story of their headship with the words: 'What I wanted was …' or 'I was determined to see that …'?

Oh, of course it's possible that these wishes and desires were based on a proper assessment of what was needed, but somehow you know that it wasn't like that in every case. Often the new headship's seen as an opportunity to put cherished ideas into action, when it might be better to spend quite a bit of time working out exactly what's needed, all the way through the institution.

Then there's the second bit of Drucker's advice – 'which are right for me?'

What he's suggesting is that the new leader should go first for things that he or she is good at.

So it might go like this. The new head, after a careful analysis of what's going on finds that the top three needs are – improved behaviour, a better system of analysing performance data, a total refurbishment of the children's toilets.

Which one would you go for yourself, and which would you delegate? The chances are, you see, that there's at least one that you know you could solve in short order, and one you're not brilliant at. So according to Drucker, you wouldn't punish yourself by selflessly taking on the one you hate. You'd go for the one that is so much up your street that you'd come out of it covered in glory within half a term. ('Dear head teacher. I just want to tell you how much all the parents appreciate the transformation you've brought about in the children's toilets. For years they've been a disgrace. Our daughter would come home in distress rather than use them. Now they're safe, easily supervised, and cleaned regularly during the day, a sign, if I might add, of the respect which you clearly have for our children's needs. For some this might seem a small thing, but I assure you ...')

Drucker was no wussy liberal. His thoughts on management were based on his recognition of the need for leadership, guidance, and, in the end, for telling people what to do. He believed in management by objectives, for example. He meant, though, objectives that were arrived at by agreement, and not imposed from outside as targets. And his suggestion that a leader should pick the areas that fitted goes with the assumption that there are in the organisation people who are capable of handling the other priorities. Leadership, in other words, involved bringing people on: 'A manager's task is to make the strengths of people effective and their weakness irrelevant.'

Finally, just one more Drucker saying. You could almost run it as a mission statement: 'To eliminate the arts from education – or worse, to tolerate them as cultural ornaments – is anti-educational obscurantism.'

Peter F. Drucker (1995) *The Practice of Management*, New York: Harper Collins.

Performance-related pay might not work

Performance-related pay moves on apace. Common sense says it works – after all, people like money, don't they? Well, maybe not as much as we think – not in school anyway.

Can't take it with you

Have you noticed that people who have a lot of money – let's say many times the amount a teacher will legitimately accumulate – tend to talk about it more than the rest of us? It keeps coming up in the conversation.

'BUPA wouldn't cover it, and there was a queue for the NHS op, so I just had to shell out the thirty grand ...'

Now all that's fine by me. You can learn a lot from people who understand the difference between one financial product and another. But let me ask you this. Do you think that a person like that has changed much over the years? No, I don't either. I think the tendency to be motivated by money will have been there at the start. (Syed Ahmed, aged thirty-one, an early participant in BBC's *The Apprentice* programme, famously said, '£100,000 salary is not enough but it's a good place to start.')

Now let me ask you something else. Do you think that Syed – or any of would-be go-getters who choose to expose themselves on shows like *The Apprentice* – is likely to have considered teaching as a whole-life career?

No, I don't either. If money is your prime motivator, then you don't go into teaching.

So why, then, does anyone think that performance-related pay will improve the quality of teaching in schools?

That's one of the questions asked by Jeffrey Pfeffer and Robert I. Sutton in *Hard Facts, Dangerous Half-Truths and Total Nonsense*.

I won't bore you with the authors' detailed demolition of the case for linking pay to performance in school – you could write it yourself. They sum it all up like this:

> ... evidence shows that merit-pay plans seldom last longer than five years and that merit pay consistently fails to improve student performance. The very logic of merit pay for teachers suggests that it won't do what it is intended to do, or do it very well.

That doesn't mean, though, that we shouldn't ever reward teachers who go the extra mile. One of my pleasures as a school governor was to find small sums with which to show our recognition of, say, a TA's work with children in the holiday, making the school garden into a rich learning resource.

The subject of one-off, or occasional payments for teachers and TAs doing something extra has arisen in a number of visits I've made recently. In one school, for example, some staff were receiving an 'honorarium' for taking part in a special project. In another, talks were going on with the authority's auditor to discover what might be possible and legal. (That's never a bad idea, by the way. We always consulted our authority.) The sums were always small, and thought of as 'rewards' or 'acknowledgements', never as 'incentives'. In fact, to suggest that anyone might be induced to work harder just to get the payments would be regarded as slightly insulting.

Pfeffer and Sutton have a neat true story that illustrates how such rewards should work. A family goes into a menswear shop for dad to buy a jacket. One employee comes forward to do the 'Suit you, sir' stuff. Another takes the kids off to a playroom. When it's time to go, the kids don't want to leave, so the couple stay a bit longer and buy more clothes. It's effective teamwork, but in a conventional sales setting, the team member entertaining the children wouldn't get commission.

In this shop, however, there's no sales-based commission. Instead, everyone in the team gets, in addition to salary, small monthly payments based not on sales but on how well they keep down the number of items lost or stolen. There are only three levels of payment – zero, $20 and $40 dollars. The amounts – importantly, they're paid in folding cash – have been carefully thought out and judged so as to bring on a smile, but not distort established working patterns – 'Rather the focus remained on the celebration of the store's achievement and the spirit of camaraderie, rather than the money.'

I've done more than my share, as a head and a chair of governors, of struggling with inadequate budgets, but never have I felt that – prodded by someone with good antennae – we couldn't afford a handy little sum to acknowledge a person's special contribution and brighten their day. If you do the same, it will be repaid to you with handsome interest, I promise. (But – let me repeat this – always check with pay section and/or internal audit.)

Jeffrey Pfeffer and Robert I. Sutton (2006) *Hard Facts, Dangerous Half-Truths and Total Nonsense: Profiting from Evidence-Based Management*, Boston, Mass: Harvard Business School Press.

It's easy to be distracted from the core activity

Good heads don't miss the details. They spot the litter, the child who's in the wrong place, the gate left open. They deal with each one, and then make a note to track the error to its source. That's obviously right – the head with that kind of eye gets a reputation and is usually admired, perhaps grudgingly.

There's a danger, though, in that the detail can sometimes take over. If that piece of litter the head spotted becomes a long drawn-out item in a staff meeting, pushing aside other agenda items, then maybe it's time to rethink priorities.

Should children change into indoor shoes when they come into school? How can year heads ensure that their children wear their ties in assembly? What is to be done about teenage girls who roll their skirts up at the waist in order to bring them alarmingly high above the knees?

It's not that such questions – each within my personal experience – are unimportant. It's more that when they come up in management meetings, everyone falls on them with such obvious relish and relief. They're more manageable, somehow, than the hard matters of school improvement. I knew a head once who shamelessly used this principle, which he called 'diving eagerly into the alluring shallows of the trivial' as a ploy to keep his governors away from anything too significant. He always claimed – the truth will never be known – that his most successful diversionary tactic was to drop into a budget-crisis meeting, at which jobs could have been at stake, the idea that all pencils, on delivery from the supplier, should at once be cut in half.

'Kept 'em going all evening', he said.

Too much of that kind of displacement activity is obviously a handicap to any organisation. It's used as one of thirteen examples in a pocket-sized manual called *A Little Book of f-Laws*, by American management thinkers Russell Ackoff and Herbert Addison. Under the heading 'The less important an issue is, the more time managers spend discussing it', they explain that the trouble lies in the way we like to talk about things we think we know about – and most of us know lots about unimportant things. 'The more something matters, the less we know about it.'

For the UK, the publishers have included comments by British management writer Sally Bibb – 'a voice from another generation, another gender and another continent'. On this 'f-Law' she adds the thought: 'Managers feel comfortable discussing trivial issues because there's less at stake.' The answer, she suggests, is to remove the fear of making mistakes. 'In the best organizations, people have no qualms about changing course, or admitting that they were wrong. The aim is to resolve an issue.'

Russell Ackoff and Herbert Addison, with Sally Bibb (2006) *A Little Book of f-Laws: 13 Common Sins of Management*, Broadoak: Triarchy Press.
Russell Ackoff, Herbert Addison and Sally Bibb (2007) *Management f-Laws: How Organisations Really Work*, Broadoak: Triarchy Press.
www.TriarchyPress.co.uk

Put your effort in the right place

Most people will be aware of the Pareto principle. You might think of it as a disarmingly simple statement of the obvious – that most of the things that happen are consequent on the actions of a relatively small proportion of the people involved – a few people earn most of the money, a few of the items in your house take up most of the space, just a few of the things your baby does keep you busy most of the time. It's fun to think of examples.

Really, though, it's a serious notion, much used in management theory because it can, when you think about it, help you decide where to put most of your effort so as to gain the most results. Does it bear close scrutiny in the school setting though?

The eighty–twenty rule

If you want a general rule for running your life and your work, you could do worse than adopt the Pareto principle.

This says, in essence, that eighty per cent of any results stem from twenty per cent of the input. Originating with the Italian economist Vilfredo Pareto in the early twentieth century, and developed in the forties by Dr Joseph Juran, the Pareto principle holds good across an enormous range of activity.

Does this eighty–twenty principle work in school? Well, let's see. Are any of the following true for you? (Don't be too hung up on the exact percentages – it's a principle, not a rigid rule.)

> Eighty per cent of disciplinary problems are caused by twenty per cent of the pupils.
> Eighty per cent of your school's success is down to twenty per cent of the staff.
> Eighty per cent of a lesson's aims are achieved in twenty per cent of the lesson.

> Eighty per cent of your staff absence is accounted for by twenty per cent of your people.
> Eighty per cent of the photocopier bill is down to twenty per cent of the users.
> Eighty per cent of the staffroom biscuits are eaten by twenty per cent of the staff.

(And so on. Add your examples, and if you have any interesting, unexpected or hilarious ones, send them in to me.)

You now want to make the eighty–twenty principle work for you. Be careful, though, because it's possible to misunderstand it. Some take it to say, for example, that you should spend your management time and effort on the twenty per cent who produce the goods. Seems plausible – but as another management guru, F. John Reh, writes on his website (http://about.com):

> The theory is flawed, because it overlooks the fact that 80 percent of your time should be spent doing what is really important. Helping the good become better is a better use of your time than helping the great become terrific.

Here's a good rule of thumb test for which side of the eighty–twenty divide you're currently in, from the American Academy of Family Physicians.

It says you're swimming against the tide with the eighty per centers when:

> You're working on tasks other people want you to, but you have no investment in them.
> You're frequently working on tasks labeled 'urgent.'
> You're spending time on tasks you are not usually good at doing.
> Activities are taking a lot longer than you expected.
> You find yourself complaining all the time.
>
> (www.aafp.org)

Did you tick any of those? What, all of them?! Get away.

Settle down for the long haul

When it comes to school improvement, it's not how you get things off the ground, but how you keep everything moving upwards in the long term. Everybody can have good ideas. I, though, keep thinking of the many relics of past enthusiasms that you see around in schools – rotting canoes round the back of the sports hall, a long-dead go-kart among the weeds near the technology block, the faded lines of a baseball pitch on the school field. They all seemed like good ideas at the time, and some of them consumed quite a lot of money and teacher time. All down to experience, is the best interpretation.

Want to make something of it?

'Don't start what you can't finish', sang Elvis Presley in the 1965 film *Paradise Hawaiian Style*. I thought of that recently after I'd chased one of the young idiots who every so often would run into our ballroom dancing class, yell a moronic comment and run out again. The other night I'd had enough, and belted off in pursuit, leaving my partner, arms akimbo, in the middle of the floor. I chased the boy down the road for a few yards until he linked up with his friends, whereupon he turned round and began to outline his position. (Or, as Alan Bennett once famously put it, 'That, at any rate, was the gist of what he said.')

Of course, I could think of no further course of action that wouldn't work to my disadvantage, so I rather feebly wagged my finger at him and walked off, surreptitiously feeling for my pulse.

Common sense, surely, says that any plan or initiative that you embark upon must contain at least an indication of how it is to be sustained, where it fits into the bigger picture, and where it might ultimately lead. And yet how often have we sat round and enthusiastically signed up to a new approach to teaching and learning, or to behaviour management, only to find a year later the whole thing limping back to square one? Here are some thoughts about it, from a document I came across on the problems of sustaining change.

The author begins by reminding us that starting on an improvement drive is the bit that's exciting and energising. Top management is heavily involved at that initial stage. However, he goes on:

> Now comes the excruciating and disciplined work to keep things going ... Delving into the bowels of the organization and messing with processes, procedures, structure, etc. is very difficult and usually not as glamorous as the initial launch. But that is where sustained improvement lies.

He then goes on to look in more detail at what's meant by 'delving into the bowels'.

First comes accountability. You cannot, this author argues, maintain improvement unless you've reviewed, and if necessary changed, the structure of who's accountable for what. That means, for example, making sure that the performance appraisal system is geared to the improvement agenda. Similarly, job descriptions may have to be modified so as to tie people to the priorities, and any promotions and outside appointments must also reflect the idea of 'living the values'.

Next there's training. It's obvious that improvement carries a professional development imperative. It can't, though, just be a one-off.

> Organisations mistakenly think that 'kickoff training' is all that is necessary, [whereas] ... kickoff training simply provides understanding of the initiative and begins the education process. Such training must never stop ... internal training will have to evolve to include consistent messages about excellence.

The rest of the piece has a familiar ring, as the author points out, for example, that enthusiastic senior managers can seem to withdraw as time goes on. 'Eventually, other business issues overwhelm the team ...'

This article wasn't written about and for schools. As a matter of fact it appears on a website for managers in the hotel and travel industry. The advice, though, works well for a school. There's clearly no future in introducing a major school improvement plan if you don't tie it to the roots of the organisation – performance management, job descriptions, staff recruitment, staff training. If all that happens is an inspirational 'launch', filled with good intent, you end up, in the author's words, with 'nice to do' when what you need is 'have to do'.

In the end, in both places – school and hotel – the problem of unsustained improvement lies in the difficulty that senior management has in being everywhere at once, rallying troops on every section of the front line. And yet, when you think about it, it's that quality, sometimes uncanny, always admired, of always being there – popping into the appropriate meeting, walking round the corner into the crucial discussion, observing the key lesson – that's one of the hallmarks of the excellent leader.

Dennis Snow (2005) 'Sustaining a customer service initiative: The need for long-term commitment'. Available online at http://www.4hoteliers.com/4hots_fshw.php?mwi=1045

Slow down and be aware of your good fortune

It's really important, in leadership, to take the time to pause and enjoy the moment, rather than letting it pass by unnoticed against a background of worries and decisions waiting to be taken. Veteran writer Kurt Vonnegut had some excellent advice about this in a radio interview.

Notice when you're happy. Remember this old song, by Carson Robison?

> The sun comes up and the sun goes down,
> The hands on the clock keep going around,
> I just get up and it's time to lay down,
> Life gets tedious, don't it?

Of course you don't. It was recorded in 1948. Life was tedious then alright. You'd better believe it.

If not the song, then you surely know the feeling. Any job, teaching included, can start to drag when you've done it week in week out for ten, fifteen, twenty years. You get cynical, says the conventional wisdom. You start to cut corners. Your partner says: 'Why go in when you're not feeling well? You'll get no medals.'

Maybe you'll hear a senior teacher say, as I once did:

'If I won the lottery, I wouldn't walk straight out of here. Oh dear no. There's stuff here belongs to me ...'

I remember someone doing a 'seven ages of teaching' sketch when we were at college. He started off prancing about the room, and progressed in stages to writing notes on the blackboard. Finally he sat with his head in hands at a desk droning: 'Turn to page thirty-five and do numbers one to seventy-eight.'

The problem is that today's teaching is so closely planned from above that the rigidity and tediousness seems to seep into the bones of the teachers, making them sadly unsure of themselves.

Look at any of the teacher chatrooms if you don't believe me. They're redolent with dissatisfaction and disillusion. That's a shame, because for me the title 'teacher' is a proud one, a lifetime badge of honour that brings with it confidence and a sense of real achievement.

Luckily, not everyone succumbs to the glums. I'm frequently privileged to walk around a school with the head or a senior colleague. Often – though by no means always – it's evident that they're enjoying the experience. They just relish everything along the way – an encounter with a site manager, some repartee with a student, a quick visit to a good lesson. What I'm observing, I realise, is the special and valuable leadership gift of being genuinely interested in, and happy for, someone else's achievements and experiences.

I thought of this when I heard the writer Kurt Vonnegut, who was interviewed at the age of eighty-three, on BBC Radio Four's *Front Row*. Towards the end, interviewer Mark Lawson asked him if he found life hard.

'Oh yes', Vonnegut replied. 'Sometimes I feel I'd just as soon skip it all.'

But then he went to explain that something good always comes along to persuade him that the effort's worth it.

'We are all bribed by many epiphanies', he said. And what a wonderful expression that is – and what a beguiling idea, that as we grow old and tired and ready to be off, we're persuaded out of it by something good happening to us.

The trouble is though, added Vonnegut, that most of us just don't enjoy the good moments enough. We just let them pass by. His Uncle Alex, he said, felt strongly on the subject.

'He felt that what was intolerable about human beings was that they so seldom noticed it when they were happy.'

So, do you have time to notice when you're happy? One of the problems about having a responsible position in a school, or anywhere else, is that it's easy to skate through the happy bits, preoccupied with the loose remnants of the last problem and the first inklings of the next. So you walk down the corridor, trying to get your mind back from the difficult meeting you've just had with an angry parent and forward to the tricky lesson observation you now have to do. On the way you meet Nirmal, excited and bursting to tell you that he has a brand new baby sister, and that he went to the hospital to see her last night.

You smile, and say the right things, and move on. But do you mentally pause and focus and really engage with Nirmal, absorbing and reflecting some of his joy, staying in the moment with him? It's an epiphany for Nirmal, and you could be part of it. Be happy with him, stop to reflect on what a privilege it is to get paid for that sort of encounter in your working life – and maybe at eighty-three you'll sound as relaxed and funny as Kurt Vonnegut.

Help your leaders to lead

Management can work both ways. We surely all know that, even if we don't acknowledge it. After all, convincing your manager of the rightness of your case, or, better still, guiding him or her gently to the point of being convinced that they had the idea in the first place is standard workplace strategy.
The phrase used to describe this is 'managing up'.

Living dangerously

'Managing up' means wielding influence over the people above you in the hierarchy. It's a concept with many layers. At one extreme, it's straightforward bullying. 'Upward bullying' in fact is a phrase used by the authoritative website 'bullyonline.com' and there are some case studies there. It may be more recognisable, though, as manipulative behaviour by a sly, selfish, disloyal or criminally dishonest employee.

The other extreme is much more benign – it's the employee's attempt to secure the best deal for the organisation by trying to get under the skin of the leader's priorities and putting effort into making sure they're achieved. We'd like to think that in school 'managing up' usually means the latter.

One of the best sets of advice on managing up is by Jacques Horovitz. Originally published in the Indian management journal *Smart Manager*, I found it on the 'rediff.com' website. It's redolent with good sense such as: 'Turn grapes into wine: you are supposed to analyze the results of a market survey, and not be the mailman who passes the thick document full of statistics to your boss.' And

> Do not assume she knows as much as you do, but assume she can understand; so educate her. Please help, you are the expert. You

spend all of your time and that of your team on the issue. You live with data, pressure points and levers; your boss does not. She does not know more than you do.

Another writer, Steven L. Katz, compares this process with that of lion taming, which is a classic example of having to make a high profile performer look better than they might if left to their own devices. In his book *Lion Taming*, he argues that the good lion tamers – simply defined as the ones who die in their beds – don't grumble about this. They know that it's their job to be positive and manage what is, in terms of physical strength, a pretty one-sided relationship.

Most importantly, Katz points out, the lion tamer isn't there to belittle the beast, but to make it look as good as possible.

'One of the secrets of the lion tamer is to present the lion to the audience', he writes. (That pedestal is no accident.)

The key for us in school is that if the relationships are right, then people all along the line will be lining up their own skills and efforts so as to add energy to the shared mission.

Oh, and there's this bit of further good advice passed on by Steven Katz from the lion tamers: 'Remember that you never go into the cage without knowing what kind of a day the lion is having.'

Steven L. Katz (2004) *Lion Taming: Working Successfully with Leaders, Bosses, and Other Tough Customers*, Naperville, Illinois: Sourcebooks Inc.

For Product Safety Concerns and Information please contact our EU representative GPSR@taylorandfrancis.com
Taylor & Francis Verlag GmbH, Kaufingerstraße 24, 80331 München, Germany

www.ingramcontent.com/pod-product-compliance
Lightning Source LLC
Chambersburg PA
CBHW050553300426
44112CB00013B/1902